'It is a privilege to be invited to write the foreword to this innovatory and interesting book. The two authors show their passion for their professions and even more passion for how they can interrelate... [This book is] a joyous gift of reality; the reality of something that has been demonstrated in the work place and community with great success.'

— *From the Foreword by Sue Jennings, PhD, author, dramatherapist and play therapist, Glastonbury, UK*

'I can recommend this brilliant, easy-to-read, jargon-free, practical book as a useful and sensible guide for any discipline working in education with children and their families. It draws on the vast experiences of both authors by addressing how dramatherapy and family therapy can work within a multi-agency team in an educational setting. It describes to the reader how every piece of the jigsaw needs to be identified and come together for the well-being and benefit of the child, family, school and community.'

— *Sylvia Wheadon, dramatherapist, psychodramatist/psychotherapist, psychotherapy supervisor and specialist educational trainer (mental health), UK*

'As an educationist for over 40 years I firmly believe that a multi-agency approach provides a family with the expertise of a therapeutic alliance that understands a family's needs. The therapists can provide the skills and expertise to offer a family sustained change. Having worked internationally in schools as a manager, consultant and inspector I feel this multi-agency approach supports school staff and together they can offer a more holistic and valuable picture of a child and his/her relationship with the family. I have experienced this approach through my support work with a children's bereavement charity and have seen first-hand what a difference it has made to family members. The key, I believe, to this multi-agency approach is that the therapists facilitate change within the family rather than direct proceedings from the outside. In our increasingly complex society, I feel dramatherapy and family therapy have the potential necessary for healing, ensuring all the pieces of the jigsaw are interwoven.'

— *Annie Tempest, international educationalist, consultant, manager and inspector, UK*

T0299546

'This book is a clear and gentle entry point for professionals who work in either family therapy or in dramatherapy, or for those who are curious about learning more about either, to learn about these respective different approaches, and how they might together be useful in doing therapy within a school context... It takes the reader through a concise exposition of the goals of such an approach, while explicating each of the therapies simply and accessibly and showing the links between the two. The use of compelling case studies offers vivid illustrations of this work. This book should stimulate readers to investigate how they might add more strings to their therapeutic bows, in order to do the valuable work highlighted by this book.'

— *Janet Reibstein, MA, PhD, Registered Psychotherapist and Supervisor, Professor, University of Exeter, UK*

DRAMATHERAPY AND FAMILY THERAPY IN EDUCATION

of related interest

Creating Change for Complex Children and their Families
A Multi-Disciplinary Approach to Multi-Family Work
Jo Holmes, Amelia Oldfield and Marion Polichroniadis
Foreword by Professor Ian Goodyer
ISBN 978 1 84310 965 5

Arts Therapies in Schools
Research and Practice
Edited by Vicky Karkou
ISBN 978 1 84310 633 3

Music Therapy in Schools
Working with Children of All Ages in Mainstream and Special Education
Edited by Jo Tomlinson, Philippa Derrington and Amelia Oldfield
Foreword by Dr. Frankie Williams
ISBN 978 1 84905 000 5

How to Help Children and Young People with Complex Behavioural
Difficulties
A Guide for Practitioners Working in Educational Settings
Ted Cole and Barbara Knowles
Foreword by Joan Pritchard
ISBN 978 1 84905 049 4

The Big Book of Therapeutic Activity Ideas for Children and Teens
Inspiring Arts-Based Activities and Character Education Curricula
Lindsey Joiner
ISBN 978 1 84905 865 0

DRAMATHERAPY AND FAMILY THERAPY IN EDUCATION

Essential Pieces of the Multi-Agency Jigsaw

Penny McFarlane and Jenny Harvey

Foreword by Sue Jennings

Jessica Kingsley *Publishers*
London and Philadelphia

First published in 2012
by Jessica Kingsley Publishers
116 Pentonville Road
London N1 9JB, UK
and
400 Market Street, Suite 400
Philadelphia, PA 19106, USA

www.jkp.com

Library of Congress Cataloging in Publication Data
McFarlane, Penny.
   Drama therapy and family therapy in education : essential pieces of the multi-agency jigsaw / Penny McFarlane and Jenny Harvey ; foreword by Sue Jennings.
      p. cm.
   Includes bibliographical references and index.
   ISBN 978-1-84905-216-0 (alk. paper)
   1. Drama--Therapeutic use. 2. Family therapy. 3. School children. I. Pitman, Jenny. II. Title. III. Title: Dramatherapy and family therapy in education.
   RC489.P7M396 2012
   616.89'1653--dc23

British Library Cataloguing in Publication Data
A CIP catalogue record for this book is available from the British Library

ISBN 978 1 84905 216 0
eISBN 978 0 85700 451 2

Printed and bound in Great Britain

We would like to dedicate this book to all the children, families and schools, for their courage and forbearance, and the therapists and teams that strive to support them.

DISCLAIMER

Since the focus of this book has been intentionally based on our own experience, we have not been able to credit all the valuable work which has been done, and is being done, in this field. For this we apologize in advance, but it is hoped that, by reading this book, a sense will be gained of our personal contribution to the world of therapy.

CONTENTS

FOREWORD

It is a privilege to be invited to write the Foreword to this innovatory and interesting book. The two authors show their passion for their professions and even more passion for how they can interrelate. This is the most important message in this book to all those who work with children or have the interests of children at heart – how agencies can work together:

> You may gain ideas from reading these pieces to the effect that creating a multi-agency approach is an essential way of working towards addressing the well-being of schools, families and children.
>
> Whatever your situation, if you are reading this, you are, most likely, one of that ever-growing number of people who are beginning to see the necessity of addressing the needs of the individual child and his or her family on a deeper and more sustainable level. Moreover, the chances are that, like us, you believe in joining up the pieces of the jigsaw to help prevent further tragedies.

These are bold and pioneering statements, and they require us to look afresh at our working relationships, which of course will ultimately stem from our personal experiences. Traditionally everyone has worked within their own professional box and indeed ticked the boxes that are required in training and achievements. However, the boxed approach does not work: people and, especially, children fall between boxes and are neglected, ignored and often forgotten. In my own early work in education, I approached the local education office and proposed a 'half-way house' drama group for children who were not attending schools. I was laughed at and told that the number of children truanting could be counted on the fingers of one hand. With my staff team we found children who could be counted on the fingers of many hands, and that is how the Remedial Drama Centre started in Holloway, London, in the late 1960s.

We all need to talk to each other! Just as we hope that families will sit round a table and communicate, so members of different agencies need to meet together and look at common issues and how they can be addressed. We have to move beyond a 'territory-based' approach, where we feel we must guard our professional patch, and reach out to others with whom we have more similarities than differences, and where the total body of knowledge and experience can be brought together. Shakespeare knew how the whole body needed to be integrated as a whole (what a lesson for doctors who only treat one limb or organ!): 'There was a time when all the body's members / Rebell'd against the belly, thus accused it' (Menenius's speech from *Coriolanus*, Act 1, scene 1).

Dramatherapy and family therapy are ideal specialisms to relate to one other, and discover how their pieces of the jigsaw fit together: dramatherapy, which can embrace an integrated arts experience through verbal and non-verbal approaches, and family therapy, which has the heart of child health at its core. Not only does this book show how these two approaches can collaborate, it also emphasizes the importance of partnerships between schools and parents:

> As well as schools, families are part of the 'whole picture' of a child's life, and families experience challenges and pressures in emotional well-being as a unit.

The authors place their own experience at the centre of their theory and practice; they do not present us with a method that works before they have tried and tested it – it is not something deduced from textbooks and statistics. This means that we are given a joyous gift of reality: the reality of something that has been demonstrated in the workplace and community with great success.

I can only conclude by again using the authors' own words that so eloquently describe what they do and what they hope for:

We do this in the hope that it may motivate, inspire or support those of you already engaged in, or thinking of engaging in, this crucial work of helping today's children face their tomorrows.

Let us all be committed to helping children face their tomorrows.

Sue Jennings
Dramatherapist and Play Therapist

ACKNOWLEDGEMENTS

Our gratitude and heartfelt thanks go out to all our colleagues and fellow team members for their enthusiasm and validation of therapy in the inception of our work with children and families in education. The willingness of our fellow professionals to engage with a different way of conceptualizing and working is astonishing. We would like to acknowledge the encouragement of the schools and staff, in what was an innovative project, and their ongoing dedication and commitment to the children in their care. We thank our friends who have listened to us over the years and encouraged us to put pen to paper – especially Sue, Mel, Sharon and Sylvia. Special thanks go to Sue Jennings and Annie Tempest for their marathon reading sessions, advice and contributions.

Above all we appreciate the support and love of our families – Stuart, Leonie and Alexine; John, Paul, Joanne, Elizabeth and Edward – in our work and in the writing of this book, not forgetting Thomas, Freya, Stuart and Edward's wonderful drawings!

And finally we would like to thank all the children and families who have trusted us to help them; without them this book would not be possible.

FIRST PIECE

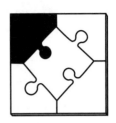

INTRODUCTION

The beginning is the most important part of the work.
[Plato]

WHO IS THIS BOOK FOR?

The chances are, if you find yourself reading this, that you are either a therapist or from the field of education, or that you care enough about the well-being and future of children to want to explore alternative and effective ways of supporting them in today's society. You may be a classroom assistant, teacher, family therapist, art or dramatherapist, educational psychologist, counsellor or youth leader, educational manager, or even someone not connected with education or therapy at all.

You may even be someone who is already part of a team that is offering a multi-agency support, in which case this book can provide additional ideas about working with children and their families. Alternatively, you might want to establish a team of people from different professions to offer an innovative multi-agency approach in supporting children which includes therapists in its makeup. You may gain ideas from reading these pieces to the effect that creating a multi-agency approach is an essential way of working towards addressing the well-being of schools, families and children.

Whatever your situation, if you are reading this, you are, most likely, one of that ever-growing number of people who are beginning to see the necessity of addressing the needs of the individual child and

13

his or her family on a deeper and more sustainable level. Moreover, the chances are that, like us, you believe in joining up the pieces of the jigsaw to help prevent further tragedies.

HOW MIGHT IT BE USEFUL?

As we have already said, this book should appeal to anyone interested in supporting children on a holistic and sustainable level. This will naturally include those already in, aiming to become part of or merely curious about the field of therapy. There are plenty of books on the separate disciplines of dramatherapy and family therapy; however, to our knowledge, there is nothing readily available which addresses both therapies within the same volume in such depth. Therefore, for anyone wishing for an overview of dramatherapy and family therapy as well as inside knowledge on how the two disciplines work together, this book provides a valuable source of information.

Furthermore, although this book expressly does *not* aim to equip the layperson to be able to work therapeutically with children and their families, it offers those already trained and qualified in the field interesting alternatives to their way of working, as well as a wealth of practical advice and examples of current practice.

It may be, however, that it is the practice of joint working rather than the therapeutic aspect which is of more interest to you as the reader, in which case the piece on multi-agency working and the case studies will provide a useful source of information on the practical issues involved in the day-to-day running of a multi-agency team.

Whether you read this book in its entirety, dip into it or study a particular piece, you may be assured that its contents have been selected specifically from the point of view of what we as therapists felt, from experience, works. On this basis, therefore, we offer this book, not as a definitive solution to supporting troubled children and their families, but as a way of working in which we believe so passionately that we wish to share its practice. We do this in the hope that it may motivate, inspire or support those of you already engaged in, or thinking of engaging in, this crucial work of helping today's children face their tomorrows.

THE CONTENTS: CONTRIBUTING PIECES OF THE JIGSAW

As therapists, qualified and experienced in our separate fields of family therapy and dramatherapy, as well as within education, we have endeavoured to make this book as user-friendly as possible by dividing it into distinct parts. These 'pieces' explore sequentially the processes of dramatherapy, family therapy, multi-agency working and joint working, before considering, in conclusion, how they come together to make up The Whole Picture. Although the pieces may be read in any order, for the sake of continuity and comprehension we advise that they be read in the order in which they appear in the book, since understanding the ethos and practice of the individual therapies is helpful when considering their joint practice and their application within the multi-agency setting.

In order, therefore, to clarify the processes and application of the two therapeutic practices, the Second and Third Pieces have been written from our individual perspectives, with anecdotes and explanations taken from our own practice, based on real experiences. The Second Piece has been written by Penny, as a dramatherapist, and the Third by Jenny, from a family therapy perspective.

Both pieces start with a definition, as we see it, of our respective professions, before giving brief explanations of some of the processes and methodologies most relevant to our work in education. Thereafter, we give a more specific account of the way that each therapy can work within an educational setting, including the practicalities of its application.

The aim of these two pieces is to introduce dramatherapy and family therapy to those not familiar with one or both, in terms that will be meaningful to a non-therapist. In this we recognize that we omit a huge amount of valuable information about both therapies and we apologize for these omissions in advance. However, since the focus of this book is to explore how therapy might work within a multi-agency team in an educational setting, we have had to restrict our information about these two therapies to that which is most relevant to this subject.

The Fourth Piece sets out to give an overall description of multi-agency working within education, including the different support provided for children, and the best ways of involving their families. It looks at some of the background components that underpin multi-agency working in general before looking at one multi-agency collaboration from its inception to its realization.

Having explained the main theories and practices underpinning the use of dramatherapy, family therapy and multi-agency working in this context, the Fifth Piece endeavours to give some insight into how the three approaches come together in joint working practice. An explanation of how drama and family therapy work together is given, as well as studies taken from our respective caseloads. In order to help preserve the authenticity of these case studies, the accounts are subjective depending on which one of us was allocated the role of key worker. The cases with a dramatherapy perspective are written by Penny, while those involving family therapy are from Jenny's viewpoint. Each case is divided under the headings 'background', 'intervention' and 'outcomes' based on the referral forms described in the piece on multi-agency working. The case allocation is stated in the intervention and, to avoid confusion, as far as possible the therapist is referred to as 'she' and the child as 'he'. We have kept to this format throughout the book except in the case studies, which are self-explanatory.

The conclusion or 'Whole Picture' summarizes our ideas on why therapy should be an integral part of a multi-agency team, and analyses the ways in which it could be useful to the child, family, team, school, wider community and within a multi-cultural society as separate, but equally important, recipients. Our final few words endeavour to sum up the ways in which we feel that the separate components of the team interlock; how, working at optimum level, the whole becomes more than the sum of its parts, and how the addition of therapy gives this whole a more intense and longer-lasting flavour.

WHY THIS BOOK NOW?
Current trends in ideology

Therapy in education is based on the belief that the creative process can help children and young people resolve their emotional difficulties and support them to be healthy and safe, to enjoy and achieve, and to make a positive contribution. These aims were the focus of UK government policy introduced to address the totality of children's lives and to ensure that all services that involved working with young people and their families were 'joined up' in meeting needs.

A key concept that has influenced political beliefs in the UK since the 1940s is that the state would look after children. *Every Child Matters* (Department for Education and Skills (DfES 2004) is the current trend in thinking about the needs of children that reflects the beliefs and values of our society that we live in now. The welfare of children is paramount, and this philosophy underpins various legislative acts and reforms that have attempted over the years to address the provision of education and health services.

The educational needs of children are built around the principles that children receive a mandatory curriculum in schools up to the age of 16 and that every child's progress is assessed. Ongoing assessment of levels of attainment in learning takes place throughout the child's life in an educational setting that reflects the current principles of social justice and inclusion. Current core values in the education of our children include aspirations to encourage attendance and avoid exclusions. The inclusive aspect of education incorporates the ideological belief that outcomes for learners are essential, rather than measuring teacher inputs.

However, testing children just on academic achievements is a limitation; assessments now include an awareness of any concerns held by educational staff about a child's physical and mental health needs besides their attainment levels. Pastoral care requires teachers to be responsible for the personal and social well-being of children in their care and to give guidance and advice on behaviour and discipline. Teachers and support staff face constant pressures to raise standards in core subjects, and to be responsible for children at risk of not achieving. Happy children achieve better, and any significant concerns about a child's emotional and behavioural well-being that cannot be met in school are dealt with by various clinicians, therapists and health professionals responsible for child health care.

Parental responsibility is incorporated in the current legislation about children's welfare. Children are deemed best looked after and cared for within their own family unit, and most parents strive to care for and be responsible for the welfare of their children. As well as schools, families are part of the 'whole picture' of a child's life, and families experience challenges and pressures in emotional well-being as a unit. Support for the family is dealt with by a range of social and health care provisions that includes family therapy.

Health clinicians working with children and families operate traditionally within their 'specialist' services. Changes to children's services require local councils responsible for child protection, safety and well-being to merge service provisions for children, resulting in many 'joined up' services and multi-agency provisions. The current trend in thinking about any provision for children and families is that it should be joined up as much as possible, and for the agencies involved to collaborate and help each other in supporting children. A multi-agency approach is part of the prevalent social economic and political culture in which we live, and therapy is a key part of collective provision, with therapists working together with other professionals in multi-agency teams.

In our opinion teams and collections of different professionals that offer an integrated service to children, families and schools need to include therapists, because they can bring a therapeutic culture to education, support children and families in direct work, and contribute a healing and positive contribution to the ethos of a team. In the following pieces we hope to demonstrate elements of these strands of a multi-agency approach and illustrate the role of therapy in education.

A brief history of therapy within education

Therapy in general has played a part within education since the 1930s, with occupational therapists working to support children with diverse learning needs through activities associated with self-care and emotional development. Other creative therapies have evolved over the ensuing years, such as dance, music and art therapies, that offer creative outlets and support for emotionally troubled children as well as guiding them through a healing process. All these therapies may play a part in mainstream education settings or in specialist schools.

Dramatherapy has been shown to be a new and different way of providing support for children with emotional and behavioural problems, and is a therapy that offers children with particular issues a way of developing emotional stability. Since the 1990s it has been a fast-growing area, with effective practice springing up in many parts of the world.

Family therapy has a rich history that began with a scientifically based objective view of families and how they should 'behave', and the treatments that should be supplied to rectify the problems they faced. Family therapy evolved to incorporate ideas about the personal reality of each family and respect their uniqueness. Different types of family therapy began to develop, and family therapy, alongside dramatherapy, has now become part of the support offered to children with a school-related problem. This support, traditionally in a clinical setting, now takes place within schools and family homes. Family therapy and dramatherapy have many aspects in common, and, as therapists trained in those disciplines, we share the mutual ethos that underpins our work with children and families.

Ways of working with troubled children have developed through clinical and educational domains quite separately over the years and with little connection between the two. As dramatherapy developed, and became an essential element of clinical work promoting personal development and growth, it gradually became recognized as a creative contribution to therapeutic work for children in schools. To bring clinical therapeutic work out of the clinic and into the school setting has been one of the endeavours of family therapy, particularly in helping to bridge the gap between the two systems of school and family.

The following pieces will reveal the new working methods and therapeutic perspectives that have successfully contributed to a multi-agency team. These, in turn, will illustrate the feedback and evaluations that provide evidence for future reference to others who want to support children, families and schools: who may be said to be those very important pieces of our jigsaw.

WHAT THIS BOOK AIMS TO DO

One of the aims of the book is to inform the reader about the therapeutic perspectives of family and dramatherapy. We aim to illustrate how they work in helping families and children change and resolve difficulties. We describe the similarities between the two therapies and how they can link together to offer a holistic approach that addresses some of the limitations of each perspective. Another of our aims is to show how multi-agency support for troubled children came into existence and the discourses that informed the creation of similar teams. In addition we explore how one team incorporated systemic ideas and therapeutic input into the work within a school setting, drawing attention to the need to take into account the whole picture of the child, family and school. Finally, we aim to show how the makeup of team members in a multi-agency team can influence supportive practice, and, in turn, how team work can offer a more complementary package. As such, this book offers a valuable resource for an integrative way of working with children and their families.

WHAT THIS BOOK DOES *NOT* DO

As previously stated, this book does not aim to provide the necessary information or instruction to equip the novice to work therapeutically with children or families in any way whatsoever. For this, an accredited course in the appropriate therapy needs to be undertaken.

Neither do we make the claim that the practice and protocols described in the following pieces are of definitive best practice, only that they are those which we have found to be the most effective within our particular work environment. Care would obviously need to be taken by anyone wishing to emulate this practice to apply modifications appropriate to their own circumstances.

Although every effort has been made to make sure that the accounts given in this book are as true as possible, it must, however, be reiterated that it has been written *primarily from our own experience and perspective.* We have not undertaken extensive research in this field and therefore do not presume to give definitive answers. Rather, in this book we offer an example of one way of working which we have found to be so effective that we wished to present it to others, whether they are able to make a difference on an individual scale with a single child, or nationally, from a management perspective.

WHO WE ARE, AND WHY WE WROTE THIS BOOK

We are two therapists who have extensive and varied experience working with troubled children and their families over many years. Having pursued our separate careers in therapy, we came together to work jointly on several supportive and therapeutic projects, most notably the co-foundation of a children's bereavement charity which uses the creative arts to support children and their families through the process of grieving.

Jenny began life as a therapist after many years as a full-time mother of four children, first training as a person-centred counsellor and at the same time studying for a degree in psychology as a mature student. Children's cognitive and emotional development was a particular passion of hers, as well as an interest in researching the impact of primary caregivers and the influence of social and environmental factors on a child's early years. During her counselling training Jenny worked as a bereavement counsellor with young adults who had experienced complicated or traumatic losses, joining them on their journey of recovery and utilizing experiential and creative techniques to support people. During this one-to-one work, Jenny became interested in the dominant discourses that influence the way people talk about loss in our society and the appropriate ways of exploring difficult issues with children.

Jenny became a project worker in an educational setting, developing and co-facilitating group work with primary school children who were experiencing family change, divorce or separation. The project encouraged children to develop a range of strategies for coping with family changes, through storytelling and role-play. The children's resilience and desire to support other children who might be similarly troubled was inspirational, and we as adults learned so much from them.

At the same time Jenny worked as a volunteer counsellor for an agency that supported people with moderate binge eating, bulimic or anorexic tendencies. Besides one-to-one individual support, Jenny jointly co-facilitated group work with young women with issues around food, using a psycho-educational approach that supported a change in attitude towards anxiety, self-harm and distorted body image. Families and carers of those people with eating disorders were also encouraged to meet regularly to share the dilemmas that they faced daily in trying to nourish and care for troubled youngsters. Working with the two separate elements – the client and the ones who cared for them – awakened an interest in understanding families, and Jenny subsequently embarked on a Master's degree in family therapy. This systemic approach training supported individual work, helping the clients explore contextual issues and understand the meaning of the problems, unique to them and their family, around food.

Child and adolescent agency clinical placement during family therapy training provided Jenny with a rich experience of collaborative work with children and their families, utilizing evidence-based family therapy interventions. Her research thesis explored the voice of the child in therapy and within their family, often unheard because of their inexperience and underdevelopment in verbal dexterity. Children's views and opinions are sometimes overlooked in families and in family therapy, and playfulness is often missing. The opportunity to work alongside and learn from other therapists who worked directly with children in similar but different ways was the next goal.

Before joining an exciting and innovative multi-agency team, Jenny worked as a therapist for a grief support service, an organization that provided therapeutic support for grief in the family. This support consisted of domiciliary assessment visits, and weekend workshops with creative group activities, for families where there had been a significant loss. This was the first time that Jenny and Penny worked together. Visiting families in their homes and during the weekend workshops, Jenny facilitated the family group work and Penny helped the children in creative dramatherapy activities.

Penny's career began in teaching over 30 years ago when she started work as a teacher of modern languages in what was then a secondary modern school servicing a large housing estate with a high level of socio-economic problems. Her interest in helping children build resilience and self-esteem despite their surroundings may be said to have begun then, although, strictly speaking, at that time, her focus was probably more on her own survival than that of the children she taught!

With breaks for having a family, Penny continued her career in education, working first as a supply teacher at nearby primary schools and then as a teacher of French and German at a local comprehensive. It was when she realized that she was becoming more interested in the emotional problems experienced by many of the children she taught than in whether or not they had done their French homework that she undertook her first training in counselling.

A course and qualification in dramatherapy followed shortly afterwards, which was when Penny made the decision to give up teaching to pursue her dream of introducing this exciting way of helping troubled children into schools in her area. Although many schools recognized the value of such therapeutic input, they were at first reluctant to commit to commissioning it since there was no 'evidence' that it worked. It was five years later and after working in other areas of dramatherapy such as special needs drama teaching, women's groups and mental health that Penny began working as a dramatherapist in an inner city primary school.

Started as research into the effectiveness of using a psychodynamic therapeutic approach to the raising of emotional literacy and self-esteem with children who were at risk of exclusion, the project expanded to include other therapists, including an art therapist, working in three more primary schools in this socially deprived area. A subsequent evaluation of the project resulted in over 20 more schools professing interest and requesting creative arts therapeutic support. Funding was obtained, and it was with the creation of a team of nine therapists working across the city that Penny realized her dream of providing a means of effective and appropriate support for emotionally troubled children in schools in her area.

The idea of using the child's natural medium of play as supportive, restorative and curative in dealing with children with emotional and behavioural issues, especially in the field of education, was then still in its infancy, and Penny was asked to write her first book, *Dramatherapy: Developing Emotional Stability* (2005), inspired by the pathos and congruity of the metaphorical stories her troubled children gave her. Although pleased with the way that therapeutic support through the creative arts had been able to address many of the needs of children in local schools, Penny was also aware of the limitations of the intervention. No matter how much work was done with a particular child, the reality was that that child had to return to the same environment which, more often than not, was the source of their trouble. With the creation of a multi-agency support team in her area, she saw a way of being able to support the child, not only by facilitating change to his internal landscape, but also by making a difference to his external environment.

Being a member of this multi-agency team provided Penny with the opportunity of doing just that, and the uniqueness, not only of working alongside other committed professionals, but also of being able to provide effective support through joint practice with her friend and colleague Jenny, inspired them both to wish to celebrate and offer up their experiences through the publication of this book.

In short, as therapists and individuals concerned for the safety and happiness of children everywhere, we wanted to share our passion for our own therapeutic 'discipline', not only the way that it works in practice, but also the way that, by working in conjunction with, as well as supplementing, a team, this sort of joint therapeutic input can, in our opinion, provide a level of support second to none.

SECOND PIECE

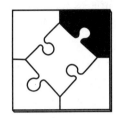

A DRAMATHERAPY APPROACH

The play's the thing
Wherein I'll catch the conscience of the King.
[*Hamlet*, Act 2 Scene 2, William Shakespeare]

WHAT IS DRAMATHERAPY?

A definition

Many people, when first faced with the concept of dramatherapy, are justifiably confused as to the difference between drama, and drama as therapy. To some it presents a synthesis of two already alarming practices: drama, when one is asked to stand up and make a fool of oneself, and therapy, where one is required to lie down and be made a fool of.

As a dramatherapist I (Penny) am often asked how dramatherapy differs from drama since, as many people have experienced, drama can improve self-confidence, promote self-esteem, provide a basis from which to explore emotional issues, and so on. The British Association of Dramatherapists (undated) explains that dramatherapy 'is a form of psychological therapy in which all of the performance arts are utilised within the therapeutic relationship' and that 'dramatherapists...create methods to engage clients in effecting psychological, emotional and social change'. The main focus of dramatherapy, therefore, lies in the *intentional* use of the healing aspects of drama and theatre as applied in the therapeutic process. In other words dramatherapy sets out to

25

empower people and help them explore and come to terms with their life experiences through activities such as role-play and sculpting, and through indirect approaches such as the use of stories, play texts, puppetry, masks and improvisations.

Dramatherapy is, in the main, based upon a series of processes that may stand alone or may become interwoven throughout the whole proceedings. For example, dramatic processes include invoking and exploiting role, dramatic distancing (which we will explore later), ritual and play. Psychological processes consider the elements of change, development, creativity and learning, and within the group process we look at, among other issues, relationships and the roles we play.

Who is it for?

For those who are terrified of both drama and therapy it can come as some surprise, therefore, that dramatherapy can be fun, non-threatening and curative, all at the same time. This makes it an excellent medium for working with children and teenagers with emotional and behavioural problems. However, this is not the only client group for which dramatherapeutic intervention is suitable. Many dramatherapists work in hospitals, in secure and non-secure settings, in prisons, alongside social services, in private care homes and community-based establishments, as well as in the voluntary sector. They work with the elderly and infirm, with young mums and pre-school children, and in palliative as well as restorative care.

With its emphasis on play, spontaneity and use of the imagination, dramatherapy can provide a relaxed approach to supporting a variety of different client groups through their own healing. As we shall see, the key to successful dramatherapeutic intervention is to start where the client happens to be, to enter into his reality and then gently suggest creative ways of extending or exploring it. With a child this may be through play; with the severely mentally impaired, it may be through mirroring and extension; and with issue-based work such as bullying, the techniques of playback and reframing may be employed. Whatever the client group, the process of dramatherapy, sensitively and skilfully applied, can provide the stage on which insight, change and healing can take place.

What issues does it address?

The issues with which dramatherapists work are as diverse as their work settings, and the length of time taken as long or short as that particular group or individual requires. Flexibility is an absolute prerequisite of this type of intervention. They may work with bereavement, loss, post-traumatic stress, dementia, drug and alcohol abuse, brain injury and mental health problems; the list continues to grow as the effectiveness and value of creative arts therapies continues to extend its field of recognition.

What is its history?

The concept of drama as a healing art is not new. The Greeks used catharsis: the purging of the emotions through the evocation of pity and fear in their theatrical portrayals of tragedy. Sue Jennings reminds us that 'dramatic ritual which can establish individual and social identity has existed for millennia in some form or other', and that theatre provides a structure which enables, through enactment, a process which can be empowering and healing for both audience and actor alike (Jennings *et al.* 1994, p.1).

It was only in the latter half of the 20th century that the profession of dramatherapy began to develop out of drama in education. Instrumental to this development was a man called Peter Slade, who, in the 1960s and against a background of emerging arts therapy groups, encouraged children to express themselves through the medium of drama. It might be said that Slade was the first to make a link between the words 'drama' and 'therapy' (Slade 1955). Meanwhile radical changes were happening in the world of theatre through the experiments made by such theatre directors as Peter Brook and Jerzy Grotowski, which resulted in actors beginning to view themselves and their art through a more flexible and therapeutic lens.

Another key player in the development of dramatherapy as a profession was Dorothy Heathcote, who, in an effective and almost magical way, consciously used drama techniques to educate and empower children, to 'bring out what children already know but don't yet know they know', but who said of her calling, 'I don't have a name for what I do' (Wagner 1990, p.13). This statement may resonate with many dramatherapists working with children in education these days, since we have all had times when we have felt we can't put a name to what is happening but that somehow the child is managing their own restorative process. As the headteacher of the primary school in which I first worked as a dramatherapist once said to me, 'I haven't got a clue what you do but somehow it seems to work.'

We now have a name for what Heathcote was doing in the 1960s, and since then dramatherapy has grown and extended into many different settings. Various models have developed including those from such pioneers as Alida Gersie (Therapeutic Story Making), Mooli Lahad (BASICPh), Renee Emunah (Self-Revelatory Theatre), David Johnson (Developmental Transformation), Robert Landy (Role Method) and Marion Lindqvist (Sesame) as well as the model that I have found most useful for working in schools – Sue Jennings' Creative Expressive Method.

Dramatherapy within education is still a relatively young profession and there is little documented as yet. Historically, Henry Caldwell Cook, best known for his book *The Play Way* (1917), was one of those who paved the way with his revolutionary approach to the teaching of English and his vision of a natural method of education. Richard Courtney was another, writing prolifically about dramatherapy/drama and education (Courtney 1987), and Sue Jennings' *Remedial Drama* (1984) was school/education based, as was much of her early work. More recently, authors such as Jo Christensen, Vicky Karkou and Lyn Tytherleigh have documented their experiences of working with children in schools (Karkou 2010), while dramatherapy in education is currently the focus of ongoing PhDs in universities in the UK such as Roehampton and Warwick and is discussed extensively in chapters in Leigh *et al.*'s book on dramatherapy in schools (2012).

Happily, the development of dramatherapy in education in terms of acceptance, appreciation and validation has been steady, although, it has to be said, this is subject as always to political climate. In terms of the future it is my sincere hope that it will continue to grow and reach those children for whom a behavioural approach is not sufficient. As a qualitative approach, it is difficult to quantify, but the profession is beginning to rectify this through new and enterprising evaluation processes. It may not be a 'quick fix' but the glue is strong!

HOW DOES IT WORK?
'Being' before 'doing'

This is probably the most difficult question to answer and one which every dramatherapist dreads being asked. It may be easiest to begin by saying how and when it does not work. In simple terms it does not work when the dramatherapist attempts to guess the problems facing her client and then, armed with an awesome array of techniques and a mound of materials, tries too hard to solve them. Walking into a first session festooned with bags of puppets, soft toys, coloured material, paints and wallpaper 'just in case' is a familiar scenario for many therapists, and it takes time to be able to reach a state of security where one is able to remain in the 'being' rather than always resorting to the 'doing'. Here it needs to be mentioned that, although this section refers in the main to a dramatherapist working within primary education, since that is the focus of this book, the thoughts and ideas expressed are equally applicable to the dramatherapeutic process in other settings.

The first and most important responsibility of the dramatherapist is, therefore, to start from where her client is rather than project on to him a perceived idea of where he might be. As one might suspect, this involves rather a lot of listening, but not just with the ears. Body language and behaviour can tell us as much about the child as can what he is *not* saying. Deciphering what the child is not saying takes time and experience in 'being' with him long enough and in a deep enough therapeutic relationship to understand his world and the medium through which he is trying to express his communication with that world. In this most fundamental ethos, as we shall see, dramatherapy and family therapy think alike, which accounts for the ease in which they achieve such a harmonious joint working relationship.

The 'doing'

Having formed a relationship and, it is hoped, a rapport with the child and having been allowed to enter his world, the next step is to use creative activities to extend that world, encouraging insight, healing and growth. These activities may vary considerably depending on the chronological and emotional age of the child, the issue itself and the severity of the child's reaction to that issue. They may, for example, involve the following:

- the sensory experience of sand, clay or water
- body sculpting (showing feelings through the shape or form of the body)
- mirroring (simultaneous copying)
- projecting (imagining that one's feelings or situation belong to a small figure, puppet or soft toy)
- doubling (speaking or acting for someone or something else)
- role-play.

With slightly older children, techniques taken from psychodrama may be used, such as:

- role reversal (swopping roles and behaving as if you were the other character)
- asking and answering from role (usually an interaction with the audience or therapist, when the actor asks and answers questions objectively but from within the role)
- empty chair (when the child will switch chairs to ask and answer questions as if he were two separate people).

And with groups:

- group sculpts (as with body sculpting to show feelings or a situation)
- freeze frames (a tableau of still positions which describe a scene or event).

This is a simple but not definitive list of techniques which I have found useful in my work in schools with children with emotional and behavioural difficulties. Depending on the particular interest and skill base of the dramatherapist, many other techniques and approaches may be used, such as sand trays, masks and performance.

Dramatherapists work with a variety of materials. More often than not a dramatherapist working in schools will have a number of lengths of material, brightly coloured and sparkly as well as black, for dressing up, and to represent not only the environment (rivers, mountains, etc.) but also the varying moods of the child. She may also have in her kitbag soft toys, puppets (the princess as well as the evil monster), small figures (animal as well as human), and art and craft materials. A typical dramatherapy session will often contain some sort of commitment to paper, perhaps as a pictorial expression of the story told previously through small figures, puppets or role-play.

Although the dramatherapist does not, obviously, work in exactly the same way as an art therapist, there are many overlaps in their methods, including the issue of directive and non-directive approaches. In spite of the differences in the creative disciplines, the underlying principles on which the therapy is based remain the same: the necessity for a safe space, the building of trust, the working through metaphor, etc. – all of which are discussed in the following sections.

The therapeutic relationship

As has already been discussed, the therapeutic relationship between therapist and child is paramount to the success of the process, as is the therapeutic alliance in the process of family therapy. This relationship has been likened to that of mother–child in that both share the underlying principles of tolerance, acceptance and respect (Winnicott 1965). In practice this means that

> the child must learn to trust the therapist as one who will provide them with the opportunities to heal and change in much the same way as the therapist must trust in the child's ability to make the necessary changes in his life if given the opportunity. (McFarlane 2005, p.1)

Johnson and Johnson (1997) argue that, for trust to develop, one or other party must let down their guard and become vulnerable to see if the other party betrays them by abusing that vulnerability. For children who have themselves been abused, this makes the development of trust a much more difficult and painstakingly longer process.

So how is this therapeutic relationship achieved? It doesn't happen overnight or 'just by magic', although there is, occasionally, something of a numinous quality attached to what happens in the space created between therapist and child. This space needs, above all, to be deemed safe, free from interruption and consistently in the same location, all of which is very difficult to achieve in a busy school environment.

Fortunately, many schools are now beginning to understand the necessity for privacy when a child is working therapeutically, but even so a recently appointed dramatherapist would do well to set out her boundaries both physically and metaphorically when starting out in a new establishment. Most unwillingness to comply with a therapist's request for privacy stems, in my experience, not from animosity but from a genuine lack of understanding. After all, current trends in school space organization have veered towards the open plan, or glass-fronted classrooms where everything and everyone is on show. Ways to overcome this lack of understanding will be discussed in the section 'How does it work within education?' on p.44.

Once a safe enough space has been established, the therapist can begin to work on trust building by 'being' with the child, as previously discussed, and accepting him as he is.

Directive and non-directive

This acceptance encompasses a way of working which is, in the first instance, usually non-directive. Most therapists, whether of art, drama or music, will wait to see what their client brings to them before using any form of directive intervention. How long this non-directive approach lasts will vary considerably depending on the style and experience of the professional involved.

As a supervisor I find that many of my newly qualified supervisees prefer to remain within the safety of the non-directive approach rather than risk pointing the child in the 'wrong' direction. In other words, they prefer to let the child remain consistently in control of the sessions and of the material they bring. For children who have been victims of adults' overbearing behaviour, it is obviously paramount not to repeat this experience in the sessions, but there comes a time when a skilled therapist has been given enough information by a child to interpret his attitude and actions and is then able to provide the appropriate means and opportunity to facilitate change.

This then becomes a 'directive' intervention, insofar as the child has been directed towards a way of working which the therapist deems most likely to bring about the most necessary healing. The child may still be in control of the content of the sessions but the therapist has taken over control of the process. For example, a child, who through undirected play with small figures has created a number of stories which seem to have a common theme of being alone in the world, may be encouraged to use the 'six-part story' method which explores the nature of the 'helper' (see the section 'Lahad's six-part story method' on p.48 for a full explanation of this activity). In another scenario, a child, who has, as the central character to her stories, a little girl who is exactly the same age as she was when her mother left the family, may be encouraged, through the use of puppets and role-play, to explore the feelings of that little girl, using a technique which dramatherapists call 'dramatic distancing'.

Dramatic distancing

Dramatic distancing has its roots in the theatre, where we experience the emotions of the actors without having to play the role ourselves. This distancing allows us to experience emotions, which might otherwise be too enormous for us, in a safe and structured way. The ability to move between two different realities, that of the fictional and non-fictional, allows us to experience the same event on two different levels: the subjective, when we empathize with the actor, and the objective, when we can comment on his actions and emotions. Jennings says: 'Through the creation of fiction and entering of fictive characters we not only understand ourselves better but are able to communicate things which we otherwise could not' (Jennings 1990, p.13).

Thus it is through creating a character or 'actor' who is 'me' but yet 'not me' that we can experience our own feelings from an objective point of view. As Jennings (1990b) suggests, this distance paradoxically enables us to experience the situation at greater depth and closer proximity.

So our little girl is able, through her character, to explore and experience the feelings she had when her mother left the family home. It may be a long time before she can bring herself to mention that her character has also lost her mother. It may be that she, eventually, will explain that the mother is 'dead', since the feelings around death are usually more straightforward than desertion and children will often use the word 'dead' in the metaphorical sense of 'dead to them'. With time and patience, our little girl may be able to bring out, air, explore and come to terms with all those buried feelings she has regarding her mother through the medium of her character. The real-life situation of her own mother's desertion may never be mentioned, and the whole process may remain within the safety of the metaphor.

CASE STUDY:
LILLY – DRAMATIC DISTANCING

Lilly was a nine-year-old girl with a disturbing history of abusive foster homes. She had left her original family at the age of three when her natural mother had produced twins. Social services had taken away all three children because of the mother's drug and alcohol problem and refusal to part from her abusive and violent partner.

Unfortunately Lilly's first foster parents, with whom she had made a strong bond, were unable to keep her, and there began for Lilly a succession of temporary foster homes while a search for a permanent placement was under way. By the age of six Lilly was a troubled child, trusting no one, prone to stealing and likely to run away at the drop of a hat. Sessions with Lilly took place over a long period of time, during which I let Lilly take control of what she did in a way that was completely different to the lack of control she felt over the succession of rapid changes in her life.

From the very first session she identified with a small giraffe puppet, rather bedraggled and with one ear missing. It had a very sad expression on its face and, in answer to Lilly's query, I told her that it was because it had no Mummy and that people had not always been nice to it. Jerry, as Lilly named him, went everywhere with Lilly from then on, and it was through Jerry that we were able to explore the feelings of anger, confusion, fear and hope that Lilly could not express herself. Finally, Jerry was able to help us make the transition into a family which eventually adopted Lilly and whom Lilly (and Jerry) at long last managed to trust.

Metaphor and symbol

It could be said that metaphor and symbol are fundamental tools of the trade for the dramatherapist, especially in education, in that they represent an alternative means of expression: one through which children, on the whole, find it easy to communicate.

Why should this be so? The developmental psychologist Jean Piaget states in his theory (see Piaget 1970) that, before a certain age, cognitive abilities with regards to the abstract are not yet fully developed, which makes the processing of abstract concepts very difficult for a small child. To be able to put an abstract concept into concrete form is very helpful; for example, for the child with special needs who can show his sadness at having no friends through a puppet which lives by itself on an island. Therefore, just as in family therapy, a therapist will search collaboratively with a family for a metaphor which more aptly describes their situation, so a dramatherapist will encourage a child to explore his situation through the use of story, symbol and metaphorical images.

So what are these symbols and images and in what way do they speak to the unconscious? To answer this question we can draw on the theories of the psychologist Carl Gustav Jung (1865–1961), on which many dramatherapeutic principles are based. Jung contended that life has meaning, and that this meaning can be understood through the unconscious in a series of symbols (Jung 1978). He believed that

> the inner world of the unconscious communicated with our ego self through a language of spontaneous images and symbols and that these images and symbols had a compensatory function counterbalancing

deficiencies or one sided tendencies of the conscious ego standpoint. (McFarlane 2005, p.10)

Jung further contended that the psyche was always striving towards 'wholeness', and that the unconscious was continually bombarding us, through dreams, daydreams and spontaneous thoughts and actions, with ways in which we can achieve this 'wholeness'.

Dramatherapy is based on the exploration of these images and symbols through the medium of creative expression, so that healing, or, to use Jungian language, 'wholeness', can be achieved. It follows, therefore, that dramatherapy might be a natural medium to use with children when trying to understand the unconscious processes which give rise to their behaviour, since they will only understand it themselves through images and symbols. In other words, many children will not be able to tell you in spoken language why they are behaving in such a way, but can show you through the metaphor of their play. After all, as the Greek author and philosopher Plato (427–347 BC) suggested, play is a more expressive medium, since you can discover more about a person in an hour of play than in a year of conversation.

The word 'metaphor', from the Greek, literally means 'to carry over', and refers to the transportation of emotionally charged images from the creative, perceptive right hemisphere of the brain where they are first 'felt', to the logical, reasoning left hemisphere, responsible for language. The left hemisphere finds a word for the image that has originated in the right, and this image, if allowed to be spontaneous and unrestricted by the usual analytical, critical functions of the left side, will be nearest to the truth of how a child is feeling.

For the therapist, metaphor can open up the possibility of a wealth of questions leading to exploration of the image and what it means to the client or child without changing external reality. Mooli Lahad (2000) gives us the example of a locomotive which his supervisee has chosen to represent her client. While many questions, such as 'Is there a driver?', 'How old is the locomotive?' and 'Is it at a junction?', can be asked to find out how the client impacts on the supervisee, this exploration does not change the immediate impression of the driving force of the locomotive nor the reality of the client.

Not only is metaphor a useful medium for the therapist in terms of preserving the reality of the situation, but it also helps maintain confidentiality. This works on two levels, depending on whether the child is consciously or unconsciously aware of the connection of the metaphor to reality. If the child is consciously aware of the link, he may prefer to remain within the safety of the metaphor in order to allow himself to explore his feelings at greater depth. Diana, aged 13, with whom I worked over a period of six months, created a long, involved story about a teenage girl who had been abused. Week by week we played through 'Karla's' history, always starting from the beginning and adding episodes, somewhat reminiscent of a soap opera. Only once did Diana allude to the similarity between Karla's story and her own by saying, with a mischievous expression on her face, 'It's a bit like me, ain't it, Miss?'

If, on the other hand, the child is only unconsciously aware of the connection between the symbolic story he is creating and his own, then the distance of the metaphor will allow him to begin to accept the meaning as or when he is ready: in other words he can begin to peel off the layers of fantasy which enclose the kernel of truth just as if he were peeling off the layers of an onion.

The creation of a fictional story, therefore, whether the connection to reality is consciously or unconsciously acknowledged, can be seen as a very useful medium in that it can act as a filter for dangerous material which may otherwise flood the unconscious and prove dangerous to the stability of the psyche.

Personal storytelling

Allowing a child to create his own personal story is an enormously helpful therapeutic technique, as is allowing a family to tell theirs. Its value is multi-faceted. Not only does it allow a therapist a non-threatening entrance into the child's world, which makes it an important assessment activity (see the section 'Lahad's six-part story method' on p.48), but also, even if the level of insight and subsequent change and healing is limited, it always offers great potential for self-empowerment.

For children who lead chaotic lives and are unwillingly witnesses to events beyond their comprehension and outside the realm of normal childish experience, this opportunity to be in a safe space and in control of their adventures is invaluable. Continual exposure to pain, violence, trauma or loss can render a child helpless, and this helplessness can take the form of learnt behaviour in mimicking the violence or, at best, in disorganized and unproductive activity. Saralea Chazan, in her book on playtherapy, says that 'for children who suffer the pain of trauma, disappointment and untimely disillusionment, the opportunity to play is a chance to revise and transform the effects of the past' (Chazan 2002, p.23).

The analogy I use (if appropriate) when trying to explain to a child what we are doing in the sessions is that of a chest of drawers whose contents have all been pulled out and thrown in a huge jumble on the floor. The jumble seems far too big to deal with in itself, but our plan is to take each item, dust it off, shake it out and put it back in the right drawer until there is nothing left on the floor. Some of the drawers we will be able to close, some will have to remain open a little and some will need to be opened and the contents looked at again in future. The big jumble on the floor will, however, have been sorted.

CASE STUDY:
NATHAN – PERSONAL STORYTELLING

Nathan had come for dramatherapy sessions following concerns by school staff that he often seemed 'out of it'. He would spend much time appearing to be lost in a daydream and not connecting at all to what was going on around him. In an exercise where I drew around his body and we coloured in his different feelings, Nathan informed me that he needed lots of colours for the head because it was 'all such a muddle'.

Nathan had lived in a variety of different places during his ten years of life, some of which had involved unpleasant experiences such as the witnessing of a hit and run accident and his mother leaving the family home. For the first few sessions Nathan took great satisfaction in doing a lot of 'sorting' of small figures into different types of animal or people. Eventually he began to use the figures to represent different people he remembered at varying stages of his life. He drew a big map of England and placed the small figures around it. Through projection and role-playing he told at times metaphorical and at times actual stories of the events he had experienced at different times of his life and in different places. He sorted these into 'good memories' and 'bad memories', always trying to remember something good about a place before he moved on to the next. From the very first, Nathan was in control of his own process, seeming to take great delight in his sorting procedures, until one day he informed me it was 'all done' and asked if he could go back to class because he didn't want to miss Maths!

Inherent in the value of personal storytelling is the role of the witness (the dramatherapist in one-to-one sessions or the rest of the group). Most young children are self-centred; that is to say, they believe that the world centres on them and they cannot conceive of the fact that something might be happening outside themselves. Very often they live through their imaginations; the world can become a very scary place when frightening thoughts of 'what ifs' and 'maybes' set a stage on which the child is playing the lead character. Fuelled by inappropriate viewing of television and computer games, this world can present as truly shocking to a small child, and the dramatherapist must become the 'unshockable' witness to his unmentionable fears in order to expose them for what they are.

The child may also be experiencing other emotions that can only be explored in the safe company of a trusted and 'unshockable' significant other. It is by daring to admit these feelings through the dramatic distancing of a fictional character that the child can have them accepted and normalized.

Feelings that have been experienced at a young age may also remain to haunt an adolescent. Working with young people who have been through parental separation, I have been surprised by how many are still, deep down, tormented by the idea that they may have been to blame for their parents' split. In the safety of a trusted group and through a fictional story, they are able to expose these irrational, but nonetheless troubling, ideas and lay them to rest not only in the head but also from the heart.

Personal storytelling has a further application in that it lends itself to a technique known to dramatherapists as 'reframing'. This technique has its origins in 'family systems' therapy and also forms an important part of neuro-linguistic programming. This technique involves an enactment of what never happened but what the actor or actors would have liked to happen in an ideal situation. The purpose of this technique is not to encourage a distortion of reality but to strengthen the inner world of the child by providing a series of alternatives to what might have seemed a 'no win' situation. By playing a series of various roles, the actors concerned are enabled to experience a difficult situation from different points of view, and can more easily suggest ways in which this situation might be resolved.

Many of the children who come to my dramatherapy sessions have, to some degree, been traumatized through the witnessing of domestic violence or unsuitable media material or the experiencing of persistent neglect or abuse. Their inner subjective world is very much in need of being strengthened. 'Reframing' in terms of allowing the child to have some control over his outer reality can be done safely and successfully through the metaphor.

Thus a common use of reframing might be to ask a child suffering from a recurrent nightmare to draw or act it out. He would then be encouraged to imagine how he would like the ending to have been and to draw or act this out. For purposes of clarification, psychodramatic techniques such as changing roles or speaking as different characters or objects in the dream may then be used. Although the dramatherapist may draw her own conclusions as to the cause and origin of the nightmare, this need never be alluded to, with the exploration and healing remaining firmly within the land of metaphorical images through which the child's troubled unconscious had been communicating. For example, Tom, an extremely sensitive boy of eight who continually took on the worries of others, shared with me his recurring nightmare of being stuck in a narrow alley way as a huge concrete ball was rolling towards him. In a reframing exercise Tom managed to stand up, put up his hands and shout 'Stop!'; I, as the concrete ball, was eventually persuaded to stop in my tracks once I was convinced that Tom really meant it. Neither Tom nor I alluded to exactly who or what the concrete ball was, but Tom has not had the nightmare since and is a much less anxious child.

We might say then that personal storytelling is an attempt to make sense of one's own life through the creation of a fictional character. The various techniques used to encourage this creation will be discussed in the section 'How does it work within education?' on p.44. This 'dramatic distancing' allows feelings to be experienced at greater depth and subsequently accepted and valued through being witnessed. Meaning can then be attached to something which, hitherto, felt meaningless.

Myths and fairy stories

We have already seen how important symbols are to the unconscious processes of a child's mind. In her book on fairy tales as symbols of the soul, Birgitte Brun writes: 'Working with fairy tales very much involves working with symbols, which, being related to the unconscious, are derived from archaic modes of psychic functioning' (Brun 1993, p.5). Therefore, through working therapeutically with the symbols in fairy tales, we can throw light on the fears, hopes and desires of which the child is only dimly aware, much less able to express verbally. Many dramatherapists use prewritten material in the form of fairy stories and myths to help a child in just such a way.

It may be said, therefore, that the objective which underpins working with myths and fairy stories is much the same as personal storytelling – that of making sense of one's life. With prewritten material, however, the main character is, obviously, already in possession of certain qualities, the events already in place, and it falls to the expertise of the dramatherapist to choose the story with the greatest potential for allegorical exploration. Care must obviously be taken to ensure that the story is absolutely appropriate and holds no hidden snares of unnecessary violence, racism or prejudice.

Two young brothers whose sibling rivalry has been causing problems in the playground and at home might, for example, be directed towards enacting 'Babes in the Wood' where they learn to pull together against a greater evil. Telling the story of and acting out 'The Ugly Duckling' can give a child with low self-esteem hope and a sense of empowerment. As Alida Gersie and Nancy King say, it is 'through identification with a hero or heroine who shows the degree of patience, wit and courage needed to surmount setbacks, [that] we learn to face our own fear and loneliness' (Gersie and King 1990, p.35).

Sometimes the choice of the story may be better left to the child since there seems to be, in my experience, inherent in the psyche, an ability to self-heal given the right conditions. The Jungian belief that the mind naturally tends towards wholeness (Jung 1978) has been borne out time and time again in my sessions where a child, when asked to pick their favourite fairy story, has chosen the one which has given the most scope for change and healing.

The same story will hold a different meaning for different children, and a child may extract a different meaning from the same story at various times of his life depending on his needs at the time. It is not so much what the story means that is important but what it signifies to the child. In this respect many therapists will admit that they are not always entirely sure what meaning a child is deriving from the material they are using, but only that, at a certain stage of the process, something numinous appears to be happening and the child moves on in his understanding and insight. It is as if 'untethered by the constraints of reality, yet within a plausible structure, our story characters explore alternative actions until an answer and way out is found' (Gersie and King 1990, p.35).

As we have already discussed, many young children find the processing of abstract concepts very difficult and, as a result, their fears may be formless and unrecognizable. These formless fears may be projected on to the archetypal fairy tale characters, explored, faced and wrestled with, all within the safety of the story. After all, it is easier to grapple with a wolf than an insubstantial black shadow.

It is not only the symbols in fairy tales and myths which provide useful therapeutic material. Myths and legends from all parts of the world and various stages in history express astonishingly similar themes. Jung explained this phenomenon through referring to the characters in the stories, not as individuals, but as symbolic representations of traits inherent in all of us. His view was that these archetypes are highly charged energy patterns of the collective unconscious which, depending on circumstance and need, we download at specific times in our lives. Thus we have all played out the wicked witch, the jealous stepmother or father, the bullying ogre, the clever magician or the childlike prince or princess.

So, in myths, legends and fairy stories, archetypal characters which are the symbolic manifestations of our instinctual behaviour play out themes which recur time after time in all walks of life, all periods of history and all countries of the world: themes such as love, betrayal, revenge, jealousy and desire. Through these archetypal themes such stories help us see that mistakes can be made in life and can be overcome. As Brun points out, 'In crises in our lives, where we tend to focus on what went wrong, the many foolish actions in fairy tales can help us reach a balance, and achieve a more tolerant and sometimes also a clearer attitude towards ourselves' (Brun 1993, p.16).

By tapping into this storehouse of knowledge, a child can be helped to feel, on a very deep level, that he is not alone, that he is part of something much bigger than himself, for which he probably has no name, but which we might call humanity. Working with adolescents with moderate to severe learning difficulties, I used the Greek myth of Theseus and the Minotaur to explore themes of arrogance, trust, betrayal and grief. As the young people enacted the final scene where Theseus, having forgotten to change the sail from black to white, was the agonized witness to his father's suicide, it was apparent, by the profound silence, that they were experiencing a cathartic reaction far beyond everyday experience. Likewise, by enacting the drawing of Excalibur from the stone in the legend of King Arthur, these same teenagers were instilled with a sense of empowerment difficult to describe in everyday language.

A sense of ritual through ritualistic action

In both the above examples, part of the power of the healing, or restorative process, was due to the fact that the enactments were witnessed (see the section 'Personal storytelling' on p.37 for an explanation of the role of the witness). In both enactments, the rest of the group watched as the main characters, Theseus and Arthur, went through a process of realization and subsequent emotional reaction. The very presence of the witnessing group imbued the scenes with a sense of ritual that added meaning and depth to the experience.

Kellermann (2000) explains that 'rituals help people to make transitions in life and to adjust to their new circumstances within a structured framework' (pp.34–35). He goes on to say that they are 'especially important in giving people a sense of safety and security and helping them express their feelings in a symbolic manner' (p.35).

Many dramatherapists have borrowed from anthropological studies to inform their understanding of the therapeutic value of ritual. Most notably Sue Jennings, writing on her experiences of living with the Senoi Temiar tribe in Malaysia, has given us an 'account of symbolic ritual in its cultural context' which helps us 'to understand the ritualization of life experiences and the implication for therapeutic practice' (Jennings 1995, Foreword).

What bigger transition is there in life than that of child to adult? And how much greater the need to give damaged or troubled children a sense of safety and security by helping them express their feelings through their own symbolic play and adjust to their new world? This is the work of the dramatherapist within the educational setting.

Further explanations as to how ritual may be used and specific applications of dramatherapy will be given below.

HOW DOES IT WORK WITHIN EDUCATION?

Since the purpose of this book is to explore how therapy works in education, the majority of the last section focused on a general explanation of dramatherapy as it might be used in an educational setting. In this section, however, I concentrate on its specific application in schools: the model used, the system of referrals, contracts with school and child and possible pitfalls, as well as the role of the dramatherapist on a multi-agency team.

'Embodiment, Projection, Role' model

As has already been mentioned, the model of dramatherapy I have found most effective for working with children in schools has been promoted by Sue Jennings and termed 'Creative Expressive'. Under-pinning this model is a process known as 'Embodiment, Projection, Role', which I consider extremely useful not only in terms of being a way of working through issues in the sessions but also as an assessment technique. This 'Embodiment, Projection, Role' (or EPR as it is known among dramatherapists) way of working corresponds roughly to the stages of child development as outlined by psychological theorists J. Piaget (1970) and E.H. Erikson (1968).

Embodiment

As a general rule the ideas of Erikson are useful background knowledge for a dramatherapist in that they emphasize the issues of conflict which may arise at a particular stage and age in life (Miller 1983). For example, in the 'embodiment' stage, which correlates to Piaget's 'sensory-motor' developmental period, Erikson states that the prevalent issue is that of 'trust versus mistrust'. This is the period when a child seeks to trust and form a healthy attachment to his primary carer. If, for whatever reason, this attachment is not made and trust is not earned, then a child may remain mistrustful, clingy and stuck in the embodiment stage, needing further sensory exploration.

Most children develop naturally through these stages, which, in chronological age, correspond approximately to birth to two years; two to five years; six or seven years; and over seven years. If, however, a child does not make a natural progression through these stages, for reasons such as illness, neglect, abuse or trauma, then the dramatherapist may need to use emotional and not chronological age-appropriate techniques to allow the child to explore this stage until he is ready to move on.

For example, Angela, although eight years old, was unable to dress up and take on a role or even use puppets and small figures onto which to project her feelings; instead she wanted to remain cuddling the soft toys and moulding the clay into unrecognizable shapes. It was only after weeks of allowing her to explore her sensory world that Angela began to want to project her feelings and tell stories with her toys.

Projection

'Projection' is the stage which I use most often as an initial assessment. Piaget explains this stage as when children first become aware of the difference between themselves and others, which normally happens some time between the ages of two and five. A child may use small figures, soft toys or puppets to explain how he is feeling by attributing them with his emotions. Thus it is more likely that a child will give an honest reply to the question 'How is Teddy feeling today?' than if he is asked 'How are *you* feeling today?'

Erikson referred to this stage as 'industry versus inadequacy', when a child is either able to project himself sufficiently into the outside world to be able to play in an industrious manner or remains inadequately enclosed in his own world. For purposes of assessment, therefore, projection is useful for two reasons: first, if a child is unable to talk 'through' the puppets or small figures, it is obvious that more work must be done in the embodiment stage for the child to begin to 'trust' himself and his environment; and second, if a child *is* able to move outside his own world and project his feelings on to his toys, then much can be learned about his world from his stories and play.

By way of assessment I often use a technique I call 'small world' which has similarities to the 'mapping' of family therapy (see the Third Piece). In an initial session I often ask a child to choose a small figure to be him and then other small figures to be the friends, family and others who make up his 'world'. By inviting him to move the figures around and place them closer or further away from each other and himself, I can gain an understanding of what may be happening for him. Further insights may then be acquired by suggesting that we make up a story with the figures. I use the word 'may' advisedly. Since all this has taken place in the metaphor, it can only be a piece of the jigsaw and cannot be regarded as fact; indeed, in terms of child protection, social services cannot act on metaphorical evidence alone. It is, nevertheless, a very useful piece of the jigsaw when trying to build a picture of the reasons for a child's behaviour.

Role

Normally, some time after the age of about seven, a child begins to see himself as others do and, according to Piaget, is able to take on another's point of view, thus opening up the magical and healing world of role-play. Before this age, trying to use role-play with a child usually proves a frustrating and fruitless experience since he is not able to see the world through anyone's eyes other than his own. This is an idea in common with family therapy's theory of mind and attachment which explains how a child learns to be empathetic to the feelings of others (see the Third Piece). Working in schools with children who come from reorganized families, we have often been asked and had to refuse to involve younger aged children simply because their role-playing of a fictional child from our story would always degenerate into very babyish behaviour. Although the improvised crying and rocking would, probably, have had some therapeutic value since they were obviously regressing to a time when such behaviour would have been the natural reaction, for the purposes of our group work it was neither the appropriate setting nor a safe enough environment to facilitate such a process. Having said this, there are, obviously, always exceptions to the rule, and I have had the experience of working with very young children who have had an aptitude for and understanding of role-play which belied their years.

Erikson viewed this stage as 'identity versus role' confusion, and this idea underpins much of the work done by Landy (1993) and his 'taxonomy of roles'. Landy was of the opinion that we all play out different roles at different times of our lives depending on the circumstances, and that one of the basic requirements of a healthy psyche is to build a fully functional role repertoire. In this, he states, dramatherapy can play a valuable part. 'Dramatherapy is most distinct among other forms of psychotherapy in that it proceeds through role. That is, both client and therapist take-on and play out roles in order to help the client discover and/or recover the most functional role system' (Landy 1991, p.7).

For children who are struggling to acquire a sense of their own identity and who, perhaps because of dysfunctional role modelling, are confused as to how they should behave in any particular situation, or who, through learnt behaviour, conduct themselves inappropriately, dramatherapy can provide an opportunity to acquire appropriate and functional ways of being in an often chaotic world.

> Through dramatherapy, different roles may be called forth, explored and either substantiated or discarded. The aim is to create a functional and viable role system where the positive and negative qualities that exist in all of us may be tolerated; to discover new ways of reacting to others which are more useful and then, through role play, to rehearse these roles in a rehearsal-for-life scenario. (McFarlane 2005, p.17)

A role repeatedly played out may be termed a subpersonality and exists to protect our vulnerable core. On the whole it is those subpersonalities of which we are not aware that have been pushed back into the unconscious, or 'Shadow' as Jung calls it, and which cause us the most problems. Through the creative, spontaneous play of the right hemisphere of the brain, these subpersonalities may be brought forth and explored, and, since they are no longer part of our 'Shadow', may become accepted as part of our whole.

LAHAD'S SIX-PART STORY METHOD

There are many activities available to the dramatherapist working with a child who has developed beyond the stage of projection and into role. One of my favourites has always been the six-part story method, which has its roots in Mooli Lahad's work on identifying coping strategies in individuals at the Community Stress Prevention Center in Northern Israel (Lahad 1992). This method was the result of an exploration into the effectiveness of a psychodynamic approach in an assessment which had hitherto only used analytical processes.

I have found this method extremely effective and have adapted it in my work with children with emotional and behavioural problems. By using visualization to create a hero or heroine, a mission, a helper, obstacles and ways of overcoming these to reach the final outcome, I encourage a child to produce from his imagination a template which may be applicable to situations in his life.

I have always found that the key to the support for the child lies in the nature of the 'helper' and signifies the way in which the child will bring about his own restorative process. Occasionally a child has difficulty in visualizing a 'helper' and thus further work may need to be done in the area of self-esteem and identity. Very often the 'helper' will be a television or computer game character; the next step then is to elicit which qualities the child perceives this character to have, and to encourage the child to embrace these qualities himself.

The six-part story method has always been, for me, a way of allowing the child to tell his own real-life fairy story. For many of the children with whom I work, life is pretty grim, but to live it without hope would be untenable. Fairy stories give children hope, especially if they are the central character.

As with many fairy stories, the 'helper' is often not of this world, as in the form of a fairy godmother. When help is not forthcoming in the real world, it is this belief in magic, in the glittering presence of someone or something that will, at the stroke of a wand, make everything better, that carries the child through. And it is within this belief in magic, which the child will probably lose as an adult, and which could be termed a link to higher consciousness, that the key to deeper understanding and acceptance of life lies.

HERO AND HEROINE

Another favourite activity involving role which I use regularly and which is reminiscent of Joseph Campbell's 'Hero's journey' (Campbell 2008) is that of encouraging a child to identify with their favourite hero or heroine. As with the choice of fairy story (see the section 'Myths and fairy stories' on p.41), the child often shows an uncanny insight into the character potentially able to provide the most scope for change, self-development and growth. Initially, I wondered at Charlotte's choice of Pocahontas as her favourite heroine, and it was only after some weeks of role-playing that I understood Charlotte's need to identify with her character's resilience and individualism. Since we often project on to others those good (and bad) qualities latent in ourselves, it is by 'becoming' and playing through our hero or heroine that we can bring into consciousness those qualities we would wish to have (and discard those we do not).

TECHNIQUES IN ROLE-PLAY

Once the choice of role has been established and both child and (usually) dramatherapist are engaged in the enactment, there are many techniques (see the section 'The "doing"' on p.30), taken both from dramatherapy and psychodrama, which can be used both to deepen the role engagement and develop insight into the situation being played out. The techniques employed will, as a matter of course, depend on the emotional age of the child, the stage of the therapeutic process and the level of potential impact on the child. All three need to be taken into consideration and are the reason why an established training course needs to be completed before such work can be undertaken with a child. The techniques in question are, for example, doubling and speaking for a character that seems stuck for words or reversing roles with the child so that he gains a fresh perspective on a situation or relationship. (This technique is very useful in dealing with learnt behaviour since a child can then 'tell himself' how he ought to behave).

Another activity which is often used in the case of unfinished business is that of the empty chair when, through repeated role reversal, an insight into how the other person may be feeling, or have felt, can be gained. (These activities are explained in more depth in *Dramatherapy: Developing Emotional Stability* (McFarlane 2005).)

USING RITUALISTIC ACTION

As already discussed, using techniques which employ ritualistic actions can be enormously useful in helping a child through a transition period and enabling them to come to terms with their new circumstances. I have often divided a room into different areas with material, and anything else to hand, to denote different times, stages or places in a child's life. Then, by slowing down the action and using repetitive questioning, a sense of understanding and 'rightness' can be gained. It is as though ritualistic actions and language help anchor us in the here and now, and rid us of projected fears about the future, as well as illusionary memories of the past. These techniques can also be used to good effect with groups: for example, as in the witnessing by a group of disabled children of an action such as the 'taking of the sword from the stone' in the legend of King Arthur. The sense of empowerment felt by each child as they take turns to draw the sword is enhanced by the slow and repetitive nature of the enactment.

In addition a child may benefit from a ritual to start and end a session, both to mark the entrance and exit into therapy, as well as to enhance the feeling of safety within the sessions. Examples of this might be a favourite song, stepping over a pretend or improvised threshold, or a particular game or visualization. When using role, the activity of 'deroling' can often provide this transition back into everyday reality.

DEROLING

The process of deroling, as developed by dramatherapists, is an important one, and is now used in many other disciplines. While much of the session may have been spent in encouraging a child to get into role, it remains an integral part of the proceedings to ensure that a child has taken off that role and is his normal self before he returns to the playground or classroom. The reason for this is obvious, especially if the child has been playing a negative character. No one needs an extra bully or monster! With older children this process can be extended into reflecting upon the character played, once the role has been 'taken off'. The extent to which a child can do this and retain or discard any particular qualities of that character shows the level of emotional maturity and literacy they have reached.

The safe space

Having explored the model of dramatherapy I find most useful in working with children, I will focus, in the remainder of this piece, on the more practical issues encountered by therapists working in schools. The first, and possibly the most important, of these is the 'safe space'. As mentioned in the section 'The therapeutic relationship' on p.31, schools often have difficulty in understanding the necessity for a completely private room, and a breakdown in relationship can occur between a therapist, who is trying to follow the protocol laid down by her professional association, and school management, who are trying to juggle the needs of their entire staff. Some schools see it as a dangerous and ill-advised practice to allow a therapist of either gender to be secreted in a room alone with a child, and many schools require the door to be left open or a glass-fronted room with no blinds to be used – a request endorsed by the British Association of Dramatherapists (2005). A reluctance to agree to these requests can sometimes result in a point-blank refusal to accommodate the therapist at all. As already mentioned, dramatherapy in education in the UK is still relatively young, and there is much work to be done to raise its profile in terms of acknowledging its value in providing not just a quick fix but a long-term sustainable change.

As I have said, much of the reluctance to engage on the part of the school may come from a lack of understanding of what dramatherapy actually does. To an outsider it may look as if the drama or playtherapist is just 'mucking around with a load of toys'. One way of overcoming this misunderstanding is for the dramatherapist to give staff training sessions which, if at all possible, should be experiential. I have found that most staff have not only enjoyed these sessions but have admitted that they have learnt a lot, sometimes about themselves!

Understandably many therapists may be apprehensive of giving a whole staff training, experiential or not. If this is the case, until the therapist knows the staff well enough to be more certain of a positive reception, consistent and thorough feedback is, in my experience, the best way to educate the staff about therapeutic intervention (see the section 'Feedback and confidentiality' on p.54).

In my first days as a dramatherapist in a primary school, I spent nearly as much time talking to the teachers and teaching assistants as I did working with the children! This may sound excessive, and obviously did not last for long, but the initial efforts paid off in terms of staff approbation and encouragement.

Contracts

In discussing the issue of contracts there are two different agreements to be taken into consideration – one with the school and one with the child. Since my time as a dramatherapist working in schools began in the days before written guidelines or protocol came into existence, I limit myself here to an outline of the way I initiated such contracts with children, but would suggest interested readers contact the British Association of Dramatherapists (www.badth.org.uk) for guidelines for best practice for working in schools.

Although it may be possible to use a straightforward written contract with an older child, there are other ways of enabling an understanding of the reason for and purpose of the sessions, which appeal more to children of all ages and which they seem to comprehend not only from the head but also from the heart. As already stated, children understand abstract ideas better when they have a concrete image in which to attach them. For example, one image I have found successful has been that of a cake. We draw the ingredients – trust, honesty, fun, etc. – and then the mixing bowl. Finally we draw the cake in the oven and agree on how long it will need to cook (i.e. how many sessions) before it needs to be assessed as to whether more time is required, or we are satisfied with the result. The drawing can be signed in the same way as would a written document and is, in my opinion, equally effective.

With regards to contracts with schools, a written agreement is obviously best practice, and I refer again to the British Association of Dramatherapists for more information on this. In brief, these contracts should cover a short explanation of the nature of dramatherapy, hours and times, confidentiality, referral procedure, parental permission, frequency and nature of report writing, privacy and room allocation, supervision arrangements, payment and accountability – especially in cases of child protection – as well as statements concerning the therapist's qualifications, affiliations, personal indemnity, tax and National Insurance.

The value of contracts both with the school and the child cannot be underestimated, since they provide boundaries and a sense of security for work which often deals with the 'unboundaried' and insecure areas of life.

Referrals

As with contracts, it is paramount that a proper procedure be established with regards to referrals for a child. Everything needs to be in writing since we are dealing with volatile and often unpredictable emotions, and I refer again to the British Association of Dramatherapists for more information on referral forms. The system of referral to which I have been accustomed usually starts with the teacher or teaching assistant (or sometimes the primary carer) holding concerns about a child. These concerns are then made known to the Special Educational Needs Co-ordinator (SENCO) in the school (or whoever is responsible for pastoral care) who fills out the necessary referral form. Referral forms vary between organizations but should, in addition to relevant details about the child, include information on specific reasons for concern, other agencies involved and, most importantly, a parental permission slip. No therapeutic work should be undertaken with a child without the express permission of the resident parent or primary carer. The legalities with regards to a non-resident parent are somewhat confusing, but I have always worked to the premise that a non-resident parent with parental rights who plays a substantial role in the upbringing of the child should be made aware of the therapeutic intervention.

In the case of multi-agency working the referral forms are then brought before the panel where they are discussed as to the most appropriate intervention, and a key worker is allocated. (This is discussed further in the Fourth Piece).

Feedback and confidentiality

It goes without saying that any therapeutic intervention in a school must adhere to the child protection procedures as laid down by the governing bodies of that school and that the person responsible for safeguarding must be consulted immediately on any issues arising. In the advent of a disclosure, best practice advises that the session be discontinued and events documented as objectively as possible. In terms of dealing with the child, some anxiety can be avoided if a discussion has taken place as to under what circumstances a therapist will need to involve another party and break confidentiality. Although this may be open to dispute, unless I have good reason to be on guard, I usually do not have this discussion in the first session since I have found that a more in-depth conversation can be had once a level of trust has been established, and that to introduce such issues too early may be detrimental to the process of trust building itself. With a younger child this conversation is sometimes more effective if done through the medium of a soft toy or puppet, as in 'we couldn't let anyone hurt…'.

As has already been said, offering as consistent and thorough feedback as possible is a good way to establish the dramatherapeutic support as a meaningful and effective intervention. This obviously must come within the boundaries of confidentiality to the client as laid down by the code of practice of the therapist's governing body. On the whole, however, I have found it helpful to remember that it is the process of the child that is of interest to other concerned professionals, not the content of the sessions. In situations concerning conflict of interest, the needs of the child must, as a matter of course, take priority.

Sole and joint working

After looking at family therapy and multi-agency working the focus will subsequently be on how dramatherapy can work alongside family therapy.

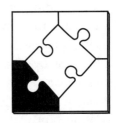

A FAMILY THERAPY APPROACH

Nobody who has not been in the interior of a family can say what the difficulties of any individual of the family may be.
[*Emma*, Jane Austen (2007, p.861)]

WHAT IS FAMILY THERAPY?

A definition

In the UK, the United Kingdom Council for Psychotherapy (UKCP) is one organization that regulated family therapy as a profession during the 1990s (www.psychotherapy.org.uk). (For current guidance see UKCP 2011). Family therapy courses had been created to establish registered practitioners in both the public and private sectors of therapeutic work, but it was during the 1950s that therapeutic work addressing families developed, and many schools of family therapy began to emerge. As such the nature of family work has been wide-ranging.

Most people these days in our society have strong views about family life and how it should be lived, and at the same time, the general public have ideas and expectations about therapy as an intervention to change families. As a family therapist, I (Jenny) will reflect on my experiences of working with families and the huge diversity and complexities I've encountered, to give a flavour of the different models and approaches that help to effect change in supporting children and their families through difficult times. Just as families are very diverse, so is family therapy, and there is no one major theory that underpins our understanding of how different types of families function. However, a primary focus within many family therapies is the idea that most human behaviour is interactive; therefore, problems can often best be addressed by helping people change the way they interact (Nichols and Schwartz 1998). Family therapy has not one clear definition, but is one way of helping people within their family systems build better relationships with each other.

Who is it for?

The family

What constitutes a family has many definitions, and the *Oxford English Dictionary* depicts a family primarily as 'a set of parents and children, or of relations, living together or not'. It goes on to describe groups, common stock, ancestors, race, kinsmen and household as some of the many features of a family. The concept of the family varies within different cultures, in religious, social and political terms, and over time. Current ideologies and discourses signify what is considered to be an appropriate mix of members or what forms a normal family unit. In my lifetime, the family myth has depicted the notion of 'two parents with two point four children', whereas demographic studies suggest that in reality families are made up of many diverse identities. A 'nuclear' family today may constitute a lone parent, gay couples, a fostering family, grandparents looking after grandchildren, or extended families and stepfamilies. Therefore a family configuration may give a sense of belonging, a way of living together that can take many forms and structures.

A family not only exists in a dimension of time, but develops over the course of time, and has a life cycle, stages and patterns (Carter and McGoldrick 1980). Living arrangements change within a household, and households themselves consist of many components and connections. Family members have roles within a family that shift over time; for example, a child is a son, becomes a father and then a grandfather, and in the course of his life takes part in many transitional and relational processes.

The system

One way of describing human activities and processes that encompass family life is to draw on a system theory. Rather than thinking of a family as a collection of individuals, one family therapy tenet views the family as a system, a whole entity in its many complexities. Although systems theory has mechanical characteristics, it is the practical explanation I focus on to outline this view of family organization and the implications for therapy.

Systems theory developed as one way of describing us all as being part of communication systems, responding and reciprocating to each other. Gregory Bateson (1972) conceived communication in terms of circularities, relying on feedback that serves to maintain a system that is stable. The components of the system co-ordinate and regulate. This explanation of what it is to be human describes systems as patterns and paradoxes of communication that are repetitive and habitual in the exchange of information within everyday human interactions. Some communications are considered contradictory and paradoxical, illustrated in the example of verbalizing a loving sentiment with a non-verbal hostile posture, so that what is meant is deemed difficult to decipher and qualify. This is termed a double binding communication. Problems within these systems of communication are maintained in patterns and rituals, and possible conflicts may easily escalate.

CASE STUDY:
CONNOR – DOUBLEBIND

A mother and her son, Connor (aged six), and daughter, Abbie (aged eight), came to family therapy because Connor kept running away from home. The mother did not know why he kept doing this, and harsher and harsher punishments had no effect.

Asking the children about their home situation, they described their mum as being really cross with their dad, who had left the family, and she was always shouting at Connor. Connor was always in trouble, and Abbie often teased him to get a reaction. Connor appeared to be in a very anxious state, being told to leave his sister alone, because the only way to retaliate to the verbal teasing was to hit his sister. He was in a doublebind, unable to both please his mother and be on equal terms with his sister, a 'no win' situation.

The mother professed to care for Connor but her tone was very repulsive. Through conversations with all three, the mother was able to realize that Connor was not his dad and that her way of talking to Connor was distressing for him to hear, and Abbie admitted that he was very easy to wind up. Through several therapeutic sessions, Connor became less anxious and didn't feel the contradiction at the heart of his relationship with his mother. He stopped running away, and although Abbie found it hard to stop teasing, Connor was able to stand his ground.

System theory also describes systems as closed, unable to adapt to elements outside of the system, or open to interaction with other systems, such as other families and the wider community. In this way the family is seen as a system responding to internal demands, as well as external challenges through multiple impacts.

The family as system

System theory evolved through various models of family therapy that had differing views of family functioning and the ways in which problems are understood, dealt with and changed. Family therapy started out as research into the way families function, and though no single grand theory emerged, different conceptual models developed. These models include structural, strategic, Milan and post-Milan, narrative and solution focused. I describe some of the models and their methods and techniques in more detail in later sections.

As systems theory evolved, the somewhat objective reality view of the family system widened to include a more subjective emphasis on each unique family, and further developed to include the views that families may be said to be socially constructed. The richness of family is echoed by the richness of the therapies developed to work with those families. The client group for family therapy is varied, and the places in which family therapy is practised are disparate as well. As one of the helping professions, family therapists work in private and public practices and are context-bound by their agency remit and ethos. Family therapy work takes place in a range of settings such as secure units with young people with mental health problems, family therapy rooms within the Child and Adolescent Mental Health Service (CAMHS), adult mental health outreach teams, marital couple work, voluntary agencies and social care. Therapy sessions may involve the immediate family unit, children, the extended family, couples or individuals. Different models of therapy may be given preference by a current agency ethos; for example, cognitive behavioural therapy is favoured by general practice facilities. My own ethical position is outlined by the term 'user friendly', that takes into account the user's experience of family therapy (Reimers and Treacher 1995).

An important aspect of therapy is the establishment of what is termed a therapeutic alliance – an important therapeutic relationship between the client and the therapist(s). Based on the premise that the therapy should fit the problem, family therapists are considering the creation of integrated therapy models, particularly ones that take into account the views of the child.

The child

Despite the view that a child is often seen as the primary focus of problems in the family, family therapy has not generally incorporated the nature of child development into its models and methodology. A child's developmental pathway is governed by genetic and environmental aspects, and two environmental aspects of child development that have a bearing on my own systemic approach are the theory of mind and attachment theory. Alongside aspects of cognitive development described by Piaget, noted in the previous piece, theory of mind depicts relational aspects of development. Baron-Cohen (1995) describes the theory of mind as the way a child develops an understanding of their own thoughts and emotions, as well as being able to imagine the minds of others, or in other words being able to 'put yourself in other people's shoes'. A young child will go through various stages of realizing that the notion of mind exists, through to understanding that their mind interprets their own thoughts and emotions about themselves. Through social interactions with others, children learn that the communication of another person and their intentions and perceptions might be different from their own.

Being able to understand what someone means and being able to look beyond the words to interpret what exactly is being communicated is an essential aspect of empathy, for example, and the ability to appreciate how someone else is feeling. Inability to understand other people's perceptions, or 'mind blindness', is one way to explain autistic traits in some children. Impairment to this mind-reading ability is another explanation for difficulties in a child's capacity to understand unwritten social rules and behaviours, as well as different styles of communication, such as sarcasm (Frith 1989).

Attachment theory defines the necessary secure attachments required for a child's development of symbolic and abstract representations in their own thinking, as well as the capacity to understand other people's thoughts. Invisible emotional bonds and attachments between a child and their primary caregiver are vital components of a secure base, requirements for the development of independence, exploring and learning about the world (Bowlby 1988). The development of emotional security is described as deriving from a secure dependence on caregivers and transforming into an ability to cope on their own.

The secure base provided in our current culture is through child–parent relationships within families, and secure attachments are associated with healthier attachment styles and social behaviour. Poor attachment patterns and problem behaviour are linked in this theory, with children who experience childhood trauma developing impaired internal working models. Although some children experience early insecure relationships, many children receive sufficient caregiving, and, if necessary, other secure attachments can be developed in future relationships.

Both these theories describe ways of describing relational and emotional development, and give some understanding about how children grow within their family environment.

What issues does it address?

Family-based interventions have been shown to be effective for a wide range of issues, and research suggests that, through these, behavioural and emotional problems for children are improved (Carr 2000). Child abuse and neglect, emotional problems, behaviour disorders and psychosomatic problems are some examples. Some family therapy approaches have focused on specific issues such as schizophrenia, while others work with couples and marital problems. Anxieties around children diagnosed with medical conditions and disorders, for example, may be issues addressed through therapeutic work with the family.

Parents also benefit from an increased understanding of their children's anxieties, resulting in a decrease in stress. An improvement in family relationships has been an integral outcome for my own work with families. Family life cycle changes, for the child, and issues such as separation, divorce and loss, for all family members, are some of the events that may affect children and their families at some time or other. The impact of these events on the family can be better understood, and any difficulties within relationships can be alleviated and eased through therapy.

The issues addressed by family therapy are as numerous as the models of interventions, but as family therapy has developed over the years, more focus has been placed on the importance of language and meaning in defining the very issues and problems that it purports to help. These two aspects are at the core of my way of working as a practitioner with children and their families, and help understand how things have come to be the way they are around family issues.

What is its history?

As a systemic practitioner I see any problems within a family as interpersonal rather than individual. Therefore systemic thinking takes into account interpersonal processes, recognizing that family dynamics have a powerful impact on individuals within the family. The history of family therapy and the development of systemic family therapy changed the focus from individual pathology, and emphasized the essential aspects of relationships, styles of communications, and patterns of experiences. For children in particular, this offered a lifeline from the double whammy of being oppressed by family dynamics as well as being stigmatized for their consequential experiences (Dallos and Draper 2000).

My own professional development as a family therapist follows a similar path to the development of the systemic family therapy approach. I began my professional therapeutic life working as a counsellor with people who suffered anxieties around eating and food. This was primarily individual work, with weekly one-to-one sessions, supporting them through a guided self-help plan within a therapeutic relationship. The 'patient' was deemed to have a condition that was a deviation from the normal, and was seen as having a problem that was specific and personal to them. The symptoms and behaviour of each client were seen as manifestations of each individual's internal state. Any progress was marked by an assessment of changes that the client was able to make to their own patterns of thinking about their problem, and to their attitude around personal control, for example. I found supporting these clients was somewhat frustrating, because the problems experienced by them seemed to be heavily influenced by their context: their family life, which seemed to be intangible and hazy and not easily understood within the counselling session. However, it was within the counselling session that their family context began to be understood; the family was where their problems and distress were often played out. Even as practitioners began working with all members of the family, dealing with different types of disorders such as anorexia, schizophrenia and depression, for example, the problems were deemed to be located within one or possibly more family members. This posited an objective and, to some extent, scientific model of working with families, and early family therapy practitioners relied on pragmatic and behaviourist methods.

Distinct schools of family therapy emerged, some of which I comment on here because they still have relevance for my practice today. Strategic family therapy, developed by Jay Haley alongside others in the 1970s, recognized that family dynamics are powerful and that transitional stages in family life are difficult for some family members to negotiate. Problems are deemed to be embedded in interactions and repetitive patterns of communications that are often unhelpful. Furthermore, problematic symptoms in one person are often maintained by other family members. Family belief systems and cognitions are also emphasized in this model, explaining that sometimes families are either exaggerating a problem or denying that something is in any way difficult at all. Strategic family therapy considers a wide range of techniques and pragmatic tasks that break up difficult sequences or patterns and offers different ways of behaving that may offer solutions for the family.

Another family therapy model that developed around this time was the structural approach (Minuchin 1974). This approach regards family hierarchies as very powerful influences that govern family life. Families are described as hierarchical structures, and these structures define who holds the power, who is in charge and who makes decisions within the family. This approach recognizes that parents need to be seen to be together in their parental decision making, because children thrive when their parents are not in conflict. Structural family therapy suggests that clear boundaries need to be maintained in family life, with parents keeping a balance between not being too 'enmeshed' or too 'aloof'. Family rules can be altered; as such, problematic behaviour can alter as well, and children will flourish.

Later developments in family therapy were influenced by the idea of social constructionism, a sociological view that social experience develops in predominant social beliefs. Family therapy models soon incorporated the meanings and the sense that families make of their own predicaments. The Milan systemic therapy approach, devised by Palazzoli and her colleagues in the 1980s, began using positive connotations in their work with clients (Palazolli *et al.* 1980). An example of this is the suggestion that each member of a family does the best that they can do. Reflecting on positive aspects of their actions with a family, a difficult behaviour may be seen as representing a strength and perhaps evidence of the different roles that each person plays in family life. These differences may be accommodated within the family and viewed as potential skills, and not problematic.

The model of narrative therapy acknowledges that communications and the meaning in conversations that people engage in when making sense of their lives is crucial. Any difficulties that they encounter and the way they are discussed often shape their choices around what to do next. Within this approach, any difficulties or problems are seen as part of a process of the way we think about ourselves and each other as problem-saturated; in other words, a particular deficiency held within us (White and Epston 1990). For example, a child would be understood as having 'internalized' a particular problem, so by 'externalizing' the problem in therapy, the difficulty becomes separate from them. In this way a person and, more importantly, a child is not seen to *be* the problem (e.g. Harry is a bully), rather the bullying behaviour is a separate factor to deal with.

CASE STUDY:
JANE – EXTERNALIZATION

Jane, an eight-year-old girl, still woke up many times during the night and crept into her parents' bed, nearly every night. This caused many difficulties for her parents, disturbing their sleep and highlighting the differences in their methods of dealing with the problem. Mum let her stay with them while Dad insisted on taking Jane back to her own bed. Jane had nightmares, and during family therapy she was described as 'a nightmare…she is a nightmare'. Her brother, aged ten, called her a 'scaredy cat'; in other words, the problem was internal.

During the first family therapy session the family members were each asked to find a different expression to describe the problem, and the family agreed that 'not sleeping' was a better description. Jane was encouraged to draw a depiction of her nightmare on a large piece of paper, and represented it as a large monster. In the externalization process Jane was encouraged to draw things that could help vanquish the monster and she drew her dad with a sword. Her brother helped draw some other things like nets and traps that could also help capture the monster. The parents joined in the drawing, and the family talked about Jane sleeping through the night, rather than concentrating on descriptions about the waking up.

With even more drawings to help and comfort her, Jane asked for the pictures to be kept by her bed each night. Subsequent meetings with the family encouraged them to talk enthusiastically about the nights that Jane was able to sleep well and how she was very brave like her dad. The family reported that Jane slept better most nights, and was now described as 'sleeping well' rather than a 'nightmare'.

Another way of encouraging a family not to view things in a problem-saturated way is through the ideas depicted in brief therapy and solution-focused therapy that emphasize competencies and exceptions, rather than difficulties and failures. Techniques include goal-setting activities that encourage more of the small changes that the family may already have made. Children in particular respond well to questions that the therapists may pose about some of the changes and exceptions that may already be happening, but may be lost in the problem-laden language used by professionals. For example, where a young girl may be described as withdrawn and anti-social, questions such as 'What do you enjoy about staying in?' or 'What would your best friend say about you doing an activity together?' would be useful. Another technique is the miracle question: 'If a miracle happened tonight, what do you think you will notice that is different?' This allows for the possibility of differences and future changes. In this approach, strategies are devised that effect specific coping strengths for families to do more of what works well in overcoming difficulties (De Shazer 1982).

Family life is often shaped by the way language is used. More recent systemic thinkers have attempted to understand the ways that difficulties are expressed through language, and therefore meaning, that people utilize in their everyday life. Family life is construed through personal identity, and self-esteem derives through the uniqueness of individual development and family experiences. As I have suggested, early attachments, and the development of attachment styles that describe the way that people relate to each other, have come to the fore in systemic work with children and their families.

Early experiences, and the way that they are described and thought about, have a particular relevance for each child within the context of their family. Therefore, words and language are crucial to the relational contexts in which they are used (Vetere and Dowling 2005).

Understanding the historical and contextual aspects of the multi-perspectives held within the family is the basis of an integrative approach to family therapy. The history of family therapy suggests that no single approach or perspective is right, but that each holds different understandings of integrated family life. Many contemporary family therapists in a systemic approach today are not 'purist' in any one approach and use an integrative model of working with children and their families.

HOW DOES IT WORK?

Systemic thinking

As described in the previous section, systemic ideas were based on the systems theory developed from a feedback proposition: the family is viewed as a system that relies on feedback, with patterns, boundaries, interactions, rules and circularities that sometimes hinder change – 'homeostasis' – or promote change – 'morphogenesis'. Therefore, any dysfunction within a family can be dealt with by outlining therapeutic strategies for dealing with any 'malfunction' (Rivett and Street 2003). My own pragmatic view is that a particular therapeutic model or intervention works if it is clinically useful at a particular moment of time with a particular family. My own stance can be construed as systemic in terms of being reflexive, collaborative and curious in joining with a family and their struggles.

Curiosity helps when first meeting with a family, and for me 'starting where the client is' – similar to dramatherapy – is one of the most important features of the collaborative process. Joining with a family and understanding their world and how they see the difficulties they are experiencing requires the therapist to skilfully listen and respond, so that a relationship or therapeutic alliance can begin to be formed. The underlying principles apply here as for all other therapies: the establishment of a contract of confidentiality, trust and the understanding that each session with a family will be a safe place to explore sometimes painful emotions. These principles will be illustrated in much greater detail in later pieces through illustrations of specific case studies.

Not-knowing

Forming the therapeutic alliance is a central feature of family therapy and requires the therapist to hold a stance of 'not-knowing' or non-expert. This can be a paradoxical position because in the later family therapy sessions the family therapist may shift from the non-expert stance to suggesting, albeit collaboratively, different interventions. However, for me, not-knowing is a good place to start when first meeting with a family. Convening a family for therapy and the process of joining with a family in the first instance involves an understanding of how things come to be the way they are for them: exploring with the family how they see their issues or problems. This understanding evolves from the therapist being non-judgemental, non-directive and respectful, as well as the essential element of curiosity. The need to remain alert and curious to the 'multitude of possible explanations and patterns relevant to the family and the family-therapy relationship' (Jones 2000, p.16) helps the therapist keep a questioning stance: exploring the description of each family member as well as being mindful of their own viewpoint during the process of therapy.

The setting

The referral process for family therapy has relevance for the way in which the family arrives for therapy and the first therapeutic session. The family have expectations, hopes and possibly anxieties about what they are about to engage in. Clinical practice settings may also have a bearing on how the therapy develops. As already noted, most family therapists work within CAMHS and work with specific issues and problems (Carr 2000). Each agency, whether public or private, will have their own mode of inviting a family to meet with a therapist. However, the initial engagement period is vital for the outcome of therapy. Where the family therapy sessions take place is dependent on the particular agency setting.

Traditionally, therapy rooms with one-way mirrors were regularly used for the purpose of training. This involved a supervisor on one side of the mirror observing a trainee family therapist meeting with a family on the other side. Co-therapy pairs, with two therapists in the room together with the family, expanded the notion of different perspectives. This practice was expanded to involve whole teams of practitioners behind the mirror observing the family. Later came the development of reflecting teams (Anderson 1990) coming into the therapy room from behind the mirror to discuss ideas with each other based on what they had observed from behind the mirror, while the therapist and family listened. The family then in turn reflect on what they had heard the team discuss. These practices were part of the development of more collaborative ways of working, the family witnessing and commenting on what is being discussed.

Generally, today, therapy sessions are one hour long, and can be attended weekly or fortnightly. However, different models, and of course agency protocols, have a bearing on the setting of therapy and indeed the process of therapy, such as how often it takes place. Certainly in the majority of therapeutic encounters, the alliance or relationship formed between the therapist and the family is central to the process.

The therapeutic alliance

Collaborative or co-joining ways of working are terms that describe the therapeutic alliance that is vital for the outcome of therapy. Together, the family therapist and the family co-construct new meanings, or new ways of describing the family and the people in that family, that is not problematic. For this collaboration to work, the therapeutic alliance needs to be established in a comfortable setting that is safe, where trust is maintained and observations are contained. The setting, another important element for the success of therapeutic work with primary school children and their families, will be illustrated in later sections in more detail.

Safety and trust do not happen spontaneously, and they are principles that have to be tried and tested through the ongoing therapy. As stated in earlier pieces, tolerance, acceptance and respect are necessary requisites. The therapist brings herself to the process of building the alliance, and during the engagement with the families she must appear authentic and respectful, able to convey her trust and belief in each family's ability to make changes. The systemic influence on collaborative therapeutic practice has highlighted the importance of language in the conversations, narratives and family stories that children and their families bring to therapy. It is necessary to adopt the language that the family use and avoid jargon-laden expressions.

Discussing the importance of the engagement of children and young people in therapy, Jim Wilson reveals the necessity of paying close attention to the use of age-appropriate language, and taking children's perspectives seriously (Wilson 2005). In this way a trusting debate can be established, where alternative strategies and ways of thinking about problems can be thought through. Wilson also advocates the idea of 'language-in-action', incorporating the same use of symbolism, metaphor and role-play as those employed by drama and play therapists using creative arts techniques. In this way the engagement of children and their families in the work of family therapy becomes more action-oriented, reminiscent of the strategies used in earlier structural approaches to family therapy, rather than just being a sedentary talking process.

Mapping

One action-oriented strategy that is derived from structural family therapy thinking is mapping. This is a way of understanding the organizational structure of a family, and can be first identified by the use of 'genograms' or family trees. Mapping, or simply drawing out the structure of the family, is an enjoyable exercise for children to participate in. Large pieces of paper and pens are necessary requirements, and children in particular enjoy the process of outlining their family tree. Where children place themselves reveals much about how they see themselves within their family, and also the importance of other family members in their lives.

A genogram is a more intricate way of mapping a family structure, because it is a visual diagram of life cycles, transition points and time lines of several generations. Usually depicting three generations, it reveals information of births, deaths, marriages, separations, divorce and the names and ages of each family member, past and present (Carter and McGoldrick 1980). Genograms are a useful tool in demonstrating close attachments or complicated and enmeshed relationships. Children and adults, too, easily identify who they are most like and who they most differ from. Careful and sensitive questioning will gain an insight of any difficult relationships and 'triangulations'. This concept depicts a child being drawn into the conflicts and arguments of his parents, for instance, and being drawn into taking sides with either the mother or the father, and perhaps even alternating between the two. This may be very confusing and distressing for the child, becoming involved with inappropriate adult conversations. Clear boundaries between the roles of parent and child may have become blurred. This problem may be addressed in a therapy session by blocking the triangulation, achieved through straightforward interpretation, and revealing a fresh understanding of a situation.

CASE STUDY: ROBERT – TRIANGULATION

Robert was the only child of Sandra, a single parent. Robert came to family therapy with his mother because he was described as 'uncontrollable' at home and disruptive at school. They lived with Robert's maternal grandmother.

During the first session, Robert, aged ten, talked about his gran, who kept telling him what to do and disciplined him all the time. Gran was invited to attend further sessions with her daughter and grandson, where it became apparent that she also kept telling Sandra what to do and how to be a 'proper' mother to Robert. Sandra was very shy and timid, and appeared to agree with her mother, but was unhappy to upset her son.

Robert oscillated between the two adult women, confused about his feelings for them both. He felt drawn towards his gran in siding with her against his mum, but was able to say that he wanted his mum to be 'harsher'. Sandra and Gran were both shocked to hear this, but his comments were unpicked to reveal that Robert wanted his mum to be consistent with her ideas about punishments and stick with them, and not change her mind and give in when Gran tried to take over. They all agreed to try out Sandra's 'fairer' ideas, and subsequently Gran reported that Sandra was earning respect from her, and Robert was much calmer.

Sculpting

Another way of mapping and understanding family structures is the idea of sculpting, a technique also used in dramatherapy. This technique involves a family member making a living structure, or sculpt, of an occasion when a problem has arisen within the family; then sculpting a time in the future when the symptoms have gone (Dallos and Draper 2000). Each family member is invited to reveal how they feel and when each one of them might feel in a more comfortable place. Physically moving people about in the therapy room is perhaps quite challenging emotionally, so one technique that I have used extensively is sculpting with stones. A selection of different-coloured stones, with different shapes, textures and sizes, are selected to represent each family member, their characters and personalities revealed through the choices that each member makes. This is a deceptively powerful technique, and the stones are a very creative medium through which strong emotions can be disclosed and ultimately change achieved.

Metaphor

Another creative medium is the use of metaphor, which opens up a wealth of ideas about change that do not immediately challenge existing realities. As described in the previous piece, the distance of the metaphor is a safety mechanism, 'like the layers of an onion' that can be carefully peeled away within the therapeutic relationship. Images and symbolism are not only an alternative way of expressing difficult feelings for children, but adults too find them an easier way to express deep emotions. Some families use metaphors a great deal, and expressions such as 'right as rain' or 'it's raining cats and dogs' have a literal and cultural meaning. Therapeutic work with children through the medium of metaphor, which reveals their choice of images, is one way to understand the reason for their behaviour problem that they may not be able to reveal at a conscious level. In a similar way, an adult may be able to describe a problem for themselves in their workplace, for example as a 'mortal combat', thus revealing the authentic depth of their feelings, and their need for 'survival' strategies. The therapist too searches for a metaphor collaboratively with the family to describe a situation together in another way that illustrates a different way of looking at a problem. Besides revealing deeper thoughts, this technique is also playful and humorous at times, and leads on to the helpful aspects of reframing, a strategic tool in therapy.

Reframing

The technique of reframing is the idea of restating a situation or problem so that it is understood in a new way. In a simplistic form this would entail regarding deafness as a gift that makes for more active listening, for example. The reframing aspects of therapy work well with children, often in the guise of a metaphor. While metaphors are deemed part of fiction and storytelling, the reframing features plausible explanations and alternative perceptions. Families often have an entrenched view of a particular difficulty and negative connotations abound. However, reframing is often surprisingly effective in thinking about 'problem behaviour' in a completely new way. For example, a girl with bulimic or anorexic tendencies may be described as strong and very determined. This was a technique that was employed in my work with people with eating disorders. Although reframing is not a panacea, it is useful in re-describing often depressing and difficult situations. It enables therapists and families to reframe acceptable meanings, thus creating a 'context for change and work with clients towards developing an understanding of the underlying meaning of their problem' (Dallos and Draper 2000, p.61).

The intention of reframing is to encourage the family to understand an alternative description of a personal or subjective problem as one that is interactional and part of the family dynamics. Families can become stuck in patterns of relating that are not always helpful, and might involve aspects of blaming. Blaming can be reframed as a wish to avoid replicating a certain learnt way of parenting, for example, and wishing to parent differently. A mother who is considered to be 'too soft' may be understood as gentle and flexible in her parenting skills. Problem-solving therapy devised by Jay Haley describes the sequences of behaviour that surround a particular problem rather than focusing on the problem alone. In his work with one family, he describes a child with a fear of dogs, and he developed a solution where the child looked after a puppy that Haley described as 'afraid of humans'. In this way the child was not only able to conquer his own fears but the family viewed him in a different light (Haley 1976).

Consideration of positive connotations for the way that family members take up certain roles in the family, such as the 'quiet one' or the 'hyperactive one', is part of the new understandings about family cohesion and how they all gel together. Shared concerns within a family become the focus of therapy, rather than fragmented individual worries. A way of ascertaining what family concerns are and how family members view each other can be gained through hearing family stories or scripts.

Family stories and scripts

Family stories are a medium through which the therapist can explore the experiences of being the eldest child or the issue of discipline within a family. Stories about past events or memories of anniversaries, for example, are ways that illuminate relationships and family values. Family secrets and generational myths can be unpicked, and, during a family therapy session, each member of the family may hear a different view of the same story. Some people perhaps become stuck or fixed on a particular way of telling a story, and in some respect re-live a particular event through their narrative, experiencing their feelings about it.

As seen in dramatherapy, the therapist becomes a witness to the personal story, but so do the other family members; while they may not be the 'unshockable significant other', they will be able to hear within the safety of the therapy session. Time and responsibility must be given in the session to manage everyone's emotions that may be revealed. Family stories are both real and fictional, and equally valid in their impact on the family. A 'misbehaving child' who is brought to therapy may hear the story of his father's 'misbehaviour' as a child through stories told by his grandmother. Validating responses from other people to storytelling enables the idea of exceptions to develop, or another way of telling the story with a different ending.

This emphasis is termed 'unique outcomes', and further therapy sessions will allow people to develop and recount stories of not doing things as well as they could rather than using the term 'incompetence'. Often-neglected aspects of narratives can be expressed (White and Epston 1990). Narratives and stories are powerful in a historical, familial and cultural extent; therefore, ways of exploring them and being mindful of different voices give some clarity to the family's idea of unity.

HOW DOES IT WORK WITHIN EDUCATION?

The previous sections have given a flavour of various approaches and techniques that are derived from the numerous models of family therapy, and I have highlighted some of the developments that have relevance for my own practice. As already stated, my own integrative way of working draws on interventions described in the various family therapy models, and I describe my working model as post-Milan. However, the guiding principles of the Milan school of family therapy are integral to my work with families and children, and how it works within education.

Post-Milan model

Although 'post-Milan' terminology is not definitive in family therapy thinking, it is a term that I use to describe my skill base and methodology, and what follows is my own interpretation. To re-visit the historical aspect of family therapy, the earlier models have been described as 'first order', based on the assumptions that the family could be changed by techniques and interventions introduced by the therapist. These assumptions relied on the premise that the therapist was 'an active agent of change and set tasks for families that were designed to alter habitual ways of managing problems' (Rivett and Street 2009, p.51).

The development of incorporating concepts such as meaning, values and beliefs, as well as questioning the views held by the therapist(s) led on to the introduction of 'second order' theory. This implies that the therapist and the family co-ordinate together, resulting in the joining of the family system and the therapist's ideas. Multiple views or formulations are possible, and the questions that occur in therapy are deemed interventions or tasks in the process of collaborative practice. In this way any changes that the family are able to make are more likely to be maintained and sustained.

Postmodernist thoughts expand systemic thinking to take account of diversity, feminism and the social construction of family life. Power and social context become relevant, as well as the use of language. Language defines, and, as often happens in the case of children, diagnosis and labelling impact on our understanding and thoughts.

As such, the 'third order' of family therapy is recognized as ways of thinking and orientation in working with families, taking into account the influences of context and using a wider lens. However, it is suggested that the integration of previous models and ideas are part of contemporary family therapy and are the necessary elements that make up a unified whole of systemic practice.

In my own systemic practice, the core ideas of the Milan approach – hypothesizing, circularity and neutrality – are the framework on which to build an understanding of a family and their uniqueness.

Hypothesizing

An interesting way of understanding family life is to hypothesize. This method was first introduced by the Milan school of family therapy, and became one of the team's innovative techniques. Hypothesizing is a formulation that investigates or assumes a hypothesis or supposition as a starting point for describing a family problem. Contemporary practice makes use of this technique to describe how a family script has contributed to a dilemma, and how family patterns may be perpetuating that dilemma now. Hypotheses (there can be many) might be elaborations, speculations and guesses that are stated clearly to the family by the lead therapist, or one of the reflecting team, as an exploration of a situation or problem, as they see it. Checking out with the family is a way of introducing new meanings, and a way of guiding discussion with the family (Jones 2000). It is essential that the therapist keep an open mind, and is flexible in revising new ideas with the family. Obviously there is no single 'truth', and as several hypotheses are developed, an untrue or an incorrect formulation, according to the family, becomes a useful way to explore other avenues. Therefore the introduction of different views or formulations during the therapy session invites the premise that views are interchangeable, and ultimately that family patterns or dilemmas are open to change.

Children in particular tend to revel in formulations that are playful, and even fanciful, as a way of alleviating what is often considered to be a 'harsh' view of themselves often provided by the school or family. For example, a child might be considered to be 'controlling' within the family when trying to order his younger sister about. I might wonder that he is trying out independent ways of behaving in becoming a grown up and perhaps he needs a crown to signify his higher status in the family. On a more thoughtful note, it might be considered that he takes his place in the family seriously because his father has left and he needs to assert himself as the only male in the household, or that he is vying to try out his independent nature. This is a simple example of the beginning process of therapy, and will enable the development of the co-construction of mutual understandings. Hypotheses are merely a temporary way of expressing ideas, and in systemic terms involve the notion of circularity. In other words, patterns in families are deemed to be circular rather than linear, more than just cause and effect.

Circularity

As a systemic therapist I understand that family patterns and interactions are relational and circular, responding to feedback. Besides being an exchange of meaning, feedback is an idea posited from systems theory that families are interacting parts or components that form the family unit. However, rather than a mechanistic view, families are seen as having emergent properties; in other words, they are part of a creative process that is evolving (Dallos and Draper 2000). Although a family may feel stuck, they are influencing and relating to each other, in circularities. Circular interactions are described as a relationship linked to a behaviour connected to another relationship, and linked to the 'problem' behaviour. An example is a mother and son who have a close relationship: the child does not want to go to school; the mother and father argue; and the child then misbehaves. A hypothesis about this 'problem' behaviour might be that the child is worried about his mother's health and that she will only be well if he stays with her. Thus a blaming linear causation of the mother's close relationship and the child's misbehaving is avoided, and an alternative formulation is expressed to understand a difficult behaviour.

Linear explanations are often couched in blaming language, referring to personality traits, whereas circularities are expressed in language that captures larger interrelated patterns. Circularities are repetitive and, within a family, serve to maintain certain patterns that may become difficult and unhelpful to a peaceful family life. Circular questioning by the therapist is a way to generate information with the family and follow their feedback. For example, questions that ask

'Who understands about coming here today?', 'How do you see the problem?' and 'Who shows their worries the most?' are all contextual queries about the family and their engagement with therapy. In this way, circular questioning has a liberating effect on the family, enabling them to be more aware of their own circularities and hence think of their difficulties from a different perspective (Tomm 1988). Other examples of circular questioning relate to future contexts, and explore the possibilities of change. For instance, 'What would you notice?', 'How will you know?' and 'What will have to happen?' are encouraging ways to think not only of alternatives but also future possibilities.

Ranking questions, in particular, a technique borrowed from strategic therapy, are enjoyed by children and adults in equal measure. For example, enquiring about feeling happier – 'Where would you put yourself on a scale of 1–10?' and 'Where do you put your brother?' – invites reflexivity for each family member, and can be fun to take part in. Scaling is a technique that reveals personal reflections and invites comparisons too. As we know, verbalizing thoughts and feelings is sometimes difficult, and the scales can be drawn out on paper and each family member invited to contribute, thus defusing the focus. An action-oriented technique would be to encourage the children to line themselves up in rank order, in terms of who is the quietest, the loudest and so on. This obviously works well with a family with several people attending the session, and relies on the supportive aspect of the therapeutic alliance.

Neutrality

Within the Milan approach, this term in its simplest form denotes a way that the therapist needs to resist alliances with family members, to refrain from linear thinking and entanglements (Hoffman 1988). As a therapist who partakes in regular supervision, it is a fundamental aspect of my practice to remain neutral and not take sides. However, in some ways this is contrary to collaborative practice, and another more helpful way of describing neutrality is curiosity, described in the previous section, that requires a non-judgemental awareness essential to an interest in all the beliefs and views of each family member.

However, a technique such as punctuation is a deliberate choosing of one point of view and checking out for relevance with other members of the family. Punctuation is sometimes demonstrated in everyday interactions as a point in which a circularity, or sequence of events, is interrupted; this highlights a particular aspect to give it a certain meaning. This may take place within family patterns, with one person responding to, and interpreting, a behaviour in a way that gives it a certain re-enforcement of meaning, thus emphasizing a moment of 'reality' or 'truth'. Punctuation might be demonstrated within a therapy session by the therapist who may notice and reflect one interaction, her view of the family reality. Punctuation entails aspects of intention, a sense of purpose, demonstrated by verbal or behavioural responses from family members, and within the therapy session by the intentional response of the therapist.

CASE STUDY:
BEN AND JULIE – PUNCTUATION

A couple, Ben and Julie, described the pattern of their conversations and rows. Julie is upset about Ben being remote and silent; Ben accuses Julie of screaming and nagging. They both describe their predictions of how they will each react, and each anticipates what they will say and do. Ben says that Julie doesn't ask him to do chores, she dictates and criticizes and 'doesn't stop talking'. Julie describes Ben as unresponsive, shut down and stubborn, walking away from the argument.

The couple, when asked to describe an argument that was different, said that everyone followed the same pattern. The pattern, as well as constructing the way they relate to each other, serves to maintain their behaviour. Acting out an argument scenario, a punctuation or difference made to the pattern acts as a deviation, and each of them responded in different ways. Julie chose different words and Ben responded, rather than remaining silent. Their motivation was clear, and they were able to make small differences when emotions were high at home. Changing the predictability, albeit with a small punctuation, created a bigger difference to their communicating patterns.

This way of communicating does not always take account of the unconscious communicating and misunderstandings that occur, that often underpin non-verbal behaviour as well as verbal reactions. Body language needs to be observed and noted. It is difficult to be totally 'neutral', and being curious about the individuals within the family context, as well as an awareness of myself as a therapist, is a more useful way of describing my therapeutic stance. An awareness of the social construction and the cultural context of family life is an essential part of my working model.

As I have already stated, I regard my defining model as post-Milan, but, as described by Elsa Jones (2000), I have difficulty in portraying a model as 'post', based on the idea of it coming after. My working model is integrative and user-friendly, and posits an awareness of what the clients require. As a systemic practitioner I am aware of families in their uniqueness and commonalities, yet mindful of the individuality of children and other family members. My therapeutic work is guided by aspects of context and secure base, two concepts that further convey my working methods.

Context

Much of the emphasis that has previously been written about family therapy has denoted the family context and the meanings attached to family rules, scripts, language and generational influences, for example. If a family is described as a system, so too are the other systems that abound: social, cultural and political systems. These systems can be described as relational and contextual, and indeed a powerful influence on how a family exists in any one time. Social constructionism 'proposes that in any given culture there are common materials, building blocks from which identities and relationships are constructed' (Dallos and Draper 2000, p.101).

Inherent in this premise is the notion of power: the idea of 'who says', and that some people in society hold more power than others. Some societies or cultures may be deemed more important or powerful at certain times. Gender identities and social realities are defined by cultural aspects; for example, in one family, describing a woman as 'only a mother' is contextually constructed within family beliefs and is also a cultural convention. In another culture 'a matriarchal mother' is someone who might be considered very powerful. Dominant beliefs and discourses influence the language and narratives that families share with each other and other families in their communities. As a collaborative therapist, awareness that the language that a family draws upon may have inherent prejudices of inequality and status is important. Strongly held beliefs about certain behaviour will be significant, and the way that language is employed to describe actions and behaviour will be crucial in how children see themselves. An example is a mother showing anger that may result in the child feeling unloved, whereby the mother decrees that displaying anger reveals how much she cares.

The use of the word 'anger' at this moment in time has negative connotations in schools, for example, and is often described as naughty, unacceptable behaviour. Another word such as 'anxiety' to describe the behaviour not only ascribes a different description and meaning for a particular behaviour, but it also has a less negative nuance. Schools too are systems, influenced by current political and social ideology, and need to be understood in that societal context. Working with the family in this way, as well as understanding children in both their family context and school context, means that a greater understanding of any difficulties emerges.

Secure base

To understand family context, a secure therapeutic base is a necessary provision to support a family coming to therapy so that they feel safe enough to explore fresh ways of relating. The term 'secure base' is derived from ideas about early childhood attachments, and it developed into a theory about a person's individual internal working model. Secure attachment styles develop from a secure base provided by a primary caregiver. Attachment styles are reflected in the way that we relate, and are relevant to systemic work with families (Byng-Hall 1995).

Attachment patterns in families are complex, and a child may have different attachment styles to each parent. The therapist needs to recognize attachment patterns that are observed within storytelling, for example. Attachment parenting styles and attachments between parents are another important aspect that impinges on a child's development and their place within the family. Exploring these family attachments are applicable to family therapy practice, and working with attachment styles will be illustrated in more depth in later pieces, but suffice to say that family-relating patterns and attachment styles are intricately linked. A secure therapeutic base (Byng-Hall 2008) within therapy may enable changes to be made within the family. My communication of sensitivity, transparency and active listening skills during the outset of a family therapy session is imperative in creating a secure therapeutic base for the family to explore new ways of relating to each other.

Systemic practice

Setting up a secure therapeutic base requires a safe space, and as already noted for all therapy, this is a necessity in establishing a therapeutic alliance with a family. Traditionally in the UK, family therapy was conducted in family therapy rooms within public institutional agency settings, and children and their behaviour problems the main focus. Family therapy has evolved to include children more within the process of therapy and to elicit their perspectives on family issues. Dramatherapy, as described in earlier pieces, has a primary creative focus and techniques that are of great merit when working with children and child-focused difficulties. Family therapy traditionally has not been a school-based service, and working with children and their families in this way has been an innovative and pioneering experience. I trained as a family therapist in a CAMHS clinical setting, working with families in a family therapy room, with live supervision from behind a one-way mirror. This was the safe place to create the therapeutic relationship with a family, a place to understand how things come to be the way they are (Jones 2000). Now, working with children from primary schools, and meeting with their families, has become an interesting exercise.

The diversity of family therapy involves working with individuals, the primary family unit, couples, grandparents and whoever attends at any one time; creating a safe space, particularly within a school setting, is equally diverse. As already described, very few schools have private and secure places for confidential work to engage with people. Practising as an outreach worker, I have worked with families in the school setting, in counselling rooms and in their homes. The context of where the work takes place has as much impact upon therapeutic work as the relational context, and an awareness of this is paramount when meeting with families.

Contracts

When first meeting with families, it is important to establish a contract with them that incorporates their understanding of what is about to take place and also the ethical guidelines that I work within. The code of practice that many family therapists adhere to is the Association for Family Therapy's (AFT) *Code of Ethics and Practice* (2011). These guidelines contain ethical requirements and principles covering family therapy as a professional practice. The guidelines also stipulate that family therapists 'promote well-being…and to do least harm'. Providing an appropriate explanation about the nature of therapy offered is an important consideration. My own family therapy work with primary school children and their families has usually been conducted with a colleague. Our first contact with the family consists of explaining that we often work together, that two heads are better than one, and that we hope to understand how they see the problem or issue so that together we may help understand these and help promote change. As part of a multi-agency team, initial contact with families comes through referrals from designated professionals within the primary school who hold concerns about a particular child in terms of barriers to learning. A more comprehensive explanation of the team and multi-agency working will follow in the next piece, but suffice to say at this juncture that the family will undertake a written permission process, and in the joining process come to have an understanding of timing and confidentiality, and some idea of family therapy work. Depending on family circumstances, and the nature of the presenting problem, the therapeutic work commences with the family verbally agreeing to the contract of work together with the therapist(s).

In the following piece, the emphasis will be on the work with dramatherapists and professionals from other disciplines within a multi-agency practice.

A MULTI-AGENCY TEAM IN PRACTICE

Take care of the sense and the sounds will take care of themselves.
[*Alice in Wonderland*, Lewis Carroll (Carroll 1993, p.90)]

WHAT IS MULTI-AGENCY WORKING?

Most children between the ages of four and eleven in the UK spend a substantial amount of time between their family unit and their primary or first schools. Both these environmental aspects of their young lives are affected by two statutory systems that have a powerful and influential impact: health and educational services. There have been legislative attempts to combine the clinicians and professionals from the many varied agencies involved in working with children. Different government acts and initiatives have been put forward to provide intervention strategies for children focusing on their family and school life, and sustainable solutions for the limitations and difficulties that young children may experience have been subjected to various aspects of the child guidance movement. Meanwhile therapeutic interventions for troubled children have been rooted in psychological and mental health provision.

This piece looks at multi-agency work and how different professions can best work together to have a positive impact on children and their families. We will look at how it works in education, the different support provided for children and the optimal ways of involving their families. First, however, we need to explain a little about the various background components which underpin multi-agency working and the systemic ethos which has influenced the setting up of one multi-agency collaboration that we were involved in from the creation.

Early identification

As suggested in earlier pieces, children presenting with a range of behavioural problems are often deemed to be the locus of the problem; sometimes families blame schools and schools blame family circumstances, and, traditionally, both may have looked towards CAMHS to provide help and support. Earlier pieces have described the way that everyday conversations and problem-saturated narratives have an objectifying aspect in defining problems, and difficult childhood behaviour is often seen as a set of defined symptoms. This view is illustrated in an audit by the Office for National Statistics (ONS) survey, stating that 10 per cent of young children in education have experienced clinically defined mental health problems (DfES 2001). However, it is often the children and their families that most need help who are least likely to access support from the various supporting agencies.

Historically in the UK, addressing children's needs, whether educational, social or emotional, has been located in the way that those difficulties have been understood and formulated, and subsequently the type of intervention that follows. Primary schools are a crucial focal point in the early years of children's lives, and teachers and other educational professionals play a significant part in a child's maturation.

Children in school

In order to learn within the primary school context, children need to have experienced sufficient support and caregiving in their family unit for them to make the necessary transition from the home environment. Life-cycle transition points are reasonably experienced when young children are coming from a 'secure base' foundation to 'where sharing, postponement of gratification, frustration and self care are to be expected' (Lindsey 2003, p.113). Some primary schools provide nurture groups to ensure a smooth transition from home to school for children who are considered to need more social and emotional support, and enhance their ability to learn (Boxall 2002). Indeed, school may be the only secure base for some children from abusive or neglectful family environments, or deprived social communities.

Young children may experience differences in culture and family values to those within the school context about expectations of acceptable behaviour, and these differing expectations are very difficult for some children to manage. The meaning and purpose of going to school, as well as how to 'behave' there, is defined by social influences and family attitudes. Family background and opinion about learning that is based on either personal failure or lack of educational success for the parents, for example, or a family history of very high educational achievers, all have an impact on a child entering the school system. The extent to which a school is able to understand the individual child and family needs will have a direct impact on how positively that school transition is experienced and for the relationship between home and school. We can therefore see that 'success' for a child in a primary school setting is determined by the understanding, compassion and support of all the adults involved.

The role of the educational psychologist

Some of these transition aspects form part of the consultancy work provided by educational psychologists, to support teachers and other professionals within the school context, through structured transition plans from early-year settings.

As suggested in earlier pieces, any psychological and developmental problems are explained by theories about individual children and their family environments. Educational psychology is an important factor in understanding a child's development within the educational environment, and educational psychologists are informed in their work with children by theories about cognitive development and learning processes, as well as the social and emotional aspects of education (Osborne 2003).

Educational psychologists are employed by local educational authorities, and some work in an independent capacity. They may work at strategic levels, as well as working directly with children, assessing their individual educational needs, or as part of a consultative provision for teachers and other professionals and parents. Direct work with children may involve observations or one-to-one interviewing to ascertain any problems, such as learning difficulties or identifying emotional and social issues. Resulting interventions might involve planning learning programmes and collaborative work with a teacher, for example. Inevitably, the culture of the school, its focus on inclusive practices and the degree of transparent and respectful communication will have an impact on the capacity for collaborative work with parents and educational psychologists in helping children.

Other key professionals

Other professionals may be involved in supporting children during their education, such as youth intervention officers and educational welfare officers, working directly with a child and their family, or indirectly within the community, addressing problems with antisocial behaviour and low school attendance, for example. These professionals, historically, have been situated within their own agencies. In recent years there have been various government legislations passed and frameworks devised to merge the supporting agencies to ensure the cohesion of support for the welfare of young people. The coming together of health, social and education services to accommodate the requirements of amendments to Children's Acts (2004, 2006) resulted in the creation of agencies and teams to offer integrated teams and co-location of services. The framework and philosophy of *Every Child Matters* (DfES 2004) proposed that key services for children and young people needed to establish new cultures and inter-agency protocols in community settings; the *National Service Framework for Children and Young People* (Department of Health (DoH) 2005) highlighted the need for imaginative and accessible methods of service delivery.

Multi-agency collaborations have emerged with different amalgamations and different groupings, such as Team around the Child (TAC), Schools Multi-Agency Resource Team (SMART) and Behaviour Support Team (BST). Some multi-agency provisions developed as teams, panels or integrated services, and some comprised as multi-professional/discipline teams, advised by the Children Workforce Development Council (CWDC). As we can see, the collaborations and projects have developed in many different ways, each one having a different definition, perspective and focus. The coming together of professionals from diverse disciplines and backgrounds has been a bumpy journey, dependent on changes in funding and resources. The ethos of joint working across professional boundaries within a school setting to support children and their families began with a pioneering collaborative approach to professionals jointly working.

Collaborative working

A pioneering systemic approach to working within schools with teams of professionals was described in the seminal text of Emilia Dowling and Elsie Osborne (1994). Health and educational professionals work jointly with both families and schools, using therapeutic strategies to deal with emotional and developmental problems in children. This was an innovative implementation of a school-based service, led by educational and clinical psychologists, for children, parents and teachers, which understood the way that both the school system and the family overlap each other. Both family and school have a perspective on a particular issue or problem, and working closely alongside supportive professionals from differing disciplines developed more productive ways to manage any difficulties experienced by a child.

In the past there has been mistrust between the family and school systems, and *The Family and the School* (Dowling and Osborne 1994) provided a systems-based theory model for working jointly with both schools and families. The model reflects the ongoing debate about the individual child as the locus of any emotional or learning problem, while taking into account the context in which the difficulties arise. Systems theory, explained in the previous piece, considers the child as part of a system, whether it is school or family, or as an individual within both systems, and, equally importantly, it understands the position of adjustment that the child experiences in negotiating between the two. The adults working within this systemic approach, whether they are teachers, educationalists or parents, understand the need to avoid unnecessary labelling and categorizing, and, instead of trying to change the child, develop strategies that change the situation and the context.

Further projects described by Dowling (2003) emphasized a school-based focus offering a consultative service for children, parents and teachers by professionals from child psychiatry and psychology services; in other words, taking the clinic to the school. The project offered drop-in facilities for parents and teachers, and individual work with a child within the school setting that understood the concerns of the teaching staff and the parents about the children's problems. Children's issues in this project included their concerns about lack of independence, bullying and feeling blamed. Other school-based projects described innovative ways of working that involved joint interventions by the different skill-based professionals, the clinical and educational psychologists, participating together in sessions with parents and group work for teaching staff.

The working practices of the clinical practitioners described by Dowling and Osborne (2003), and the projects that evolved, were underpinned by systemic thinking, and describe consultations, interviews and joint professional input for children, teachers and parents that were generally school based. These projects paved the way for some of the later school-based projects such as multi-agency support teams, particularly those established on the premise that accepting different perspectives of a problem offers different solutions and enables a collaborative approach to working with children. However, some of the multi-agency projects involved with schools focused on children's maladaptive and difficult behaviour.

Behaviour improvement

The way problems for a child are perceived and conceptualized are often defined in behavioural terms, such as inappropriate, unacceptable or attention-seeking behaviour. The Behaviour Improvement Programme (BIP) was developed as part of the Government's Street Crime Initiative in 2002, and the DfES funded 34 local authorities. Their remit was to support measures to improve pupil behaviour and attendance in some of the secondary schools and their feeder primary schools. As well as support for individual children, to promote positive behaviours and improved attendance, the measures included the use of school premises to provide a range of services and learning opportunities for pupils, their families and the wider community.

The provision of these programmes required learning support initiatives and culminated in the development of Behaviour and Education Support Teams (BESTs). These drew together relevant specialists for the planning and implementation of multi-agency approaches for vulnerable children and young people. The reduction of fixed-term exclusions and permanent exclusions was a prime consideration, and the inclusion of police officers in community and youth prevention projects in the programmes was part of the incorporation of intervention measures (DfES 2006). Drawing together specialist provision in this way formed the basis of some of the multi-agency team creations.

WHAT IS A MULTI-AGENCY SUPPORT TEAM?

In some local authorities the BIP goals included improved behaviour, reduced exclusions and truancy, raised attendance, and providing key workers to oversee the support for pupils at risk. Other initiatives involved an expansion of learning mentors in schools, and the inclusion of counsellors, art and dramatherapists' support for children, and family support workers to help the linking process between schools and families.

Inappropriate and difficult behaviour is described as one of the barriers to learning, along with emotional and social problems. The reduction to these three barriers was described as the main focus of one multi-agency BEST initiative that was developed six years ago by a local authority in the South West of England. This multi-agency support team comprised educational psychologists, family therapists, dramatherapists, counsellors, family liaison officers, primary mental health workers and community police officers from the outset. This initiative supported 25 primary schools, and the ethos required needs-led, flexible working practice. This was based on professional expertise, using preventative and reactive practice within a collaborative, systemic approach of support for schools, children and their families.

The main advantage of this approach was the multi-disciplinary expertise of the team working together with integrative theoretical and practice models. As well as working in school settings, the team had the flexibility to work in family homes and other suitable safe places, such as Sure Start counselling rooms and health centres; in other words, an outreach community team. In this way the difficulties for some children and their parents or carers to attend out-of-the-way clinics was addressed and the 'did not attend' (DNA) aspect was reduced. The collaborative, non-judgemental and transparent approach advocated by the team allowed for improved partnership with the schools and supporting professionals, as well as better co-ordination in schools between children and teaching professionals, families and teaching staff. The aim of this particular multi-agency support team service was to provide efficient, appropriate responses to requests for support from the primary schools involved in the initiative, as well as building capacity to engage in preventative work with children.

Principles

The main principles of our service centred on children and the key adults in their lives, providing both a support and a challenge function, and operating at individual, group or whole school levels. The central philosophy of efficient and open communication underscored the delivery of an effective and high quality service, offering both direct and indirect support to children, teachers and parents. The team's mainly solution-focused approach, an ethos based on identifying strengths and achievements rather than problems, identified appropriate interventions, thus ensuring the active engagement of individual children in the process of improving circumstances in the future. In addition, the team was required to contribute to the development of effective inter-agency working, through liaison with other service providers in the community, which would avoid duplication of service provision and help collaborate in the best interest of the child. All interventions from the team were rooted in evidence-based practice, and subjected to rigorous monitoring and evaluative processes, in relation to the desired outcomes of the request for involvement.

Desired outcomes

The rationale of our multi-agency support team included specific desired outcomes with evidence that the interventions of the team had a positive impact for children within the desired priorities of *Every Child Matters* (DfES 2004). Schools in the project were required to optimize collaborative working to maximize children's learning, and to participate in an inclusive ethos. Research was undertaken to provide evidence that parental views of a child's needs and their understanding of any problems were considered, and that those needs were dealt with in an appropriate and effective way. The outreach aspect of a multi-agency service was deemed to be of particular importance, and where children and families were convened and the time spent with them was of particular relevance. The results of one research project undertaken to study the impact of family therapy with children, and what they understood about the process, suggest that the setting of a collaborative service should be taken into consideration. 'How collaborative therapeutic services are implemented needs to show mutual respect of children's views, facilitating communications between children, family and education' (Harvey 2006, p.35).

Other desired outcomes for our service was evidence that schools had a more positive perception of their ability to access specialist support for vulnerable young people and their families, alongside rapid and flexible support to manage concerns they held about children.

To demonstrate how this multi-agency support team works in practice, we will illustrate a case study in the next section, starting with the referral process for an individual child, as a portrayal of the procedure of a multi-discipline team.

HOW DOES IT WORK? THE MULTI-AGENCY SUPPORT TEAM PROCESS

The process involves the following elements:

- the school completing a 'request for involvement' form
- panel discussion
- allocation of key worker role

- appropriate professional support

- contact work

- time limits and ongoing assessment

- exit strategies

- evaluation processes.

Request for involvement

The designated person in the primary school responsible for requesting support (the special needs co-ordinator or the BIP co-ordinator) fills in the 'request for involvement' form. The involvement or referral forms may vary from team to team, but in this case in point the form requires information about the child's age, school year, positive attributes, family background, and what pastoral or mentoring support has already been undertaken in school. Information is also required about specific areas of concern and the tangible outcomes of the help and support required from our team; in other words, what the work hopes to achieve. The views of the parent, and most importantly the views of the child, are included in the spaces allocated on the form. In this way the process of how the child and his family see any difficulties are included at the start. The parental permission slip for consent for any work to be undertaken with the child and family is essential, and a vital requirement before any discussion by the panel can be undertaken.

Panel discussion

A panel comprising educational psychologists, therapists and counsellors meets weekly to consider all requests for the involvement of the team. The panel team discuss priority of need and possible interventions, and then decisions are made about the most appropriate intervention and support, as well as the most appropriate professional(s) to be involved. The discussion centres on the information on the 'request for involvement' form, received from the BIP co-ordinator at the school. The panel also assess the progress of ongoing existing cases that may entail additional or change of support.

Example of a referral

In this illustrative request for involvement, Charlie, just six years of age and in the foundation or infant year of school, was described as disruptive and aggressive in class. His teacher reported that he was becoming uncontrollable at times, and she was concerned about his immaturity and challenging behaviour towards other children. At times he had tried to run out of school, and had hidden in the school toilets. His learning achievement up till now had been good but he was now starting to fall behind his peers. His mother described Charlie as a loveable child, but expressed her concerns about unmanageable behaviour at home towards his siblings, and was keen to explore the possibility of securing a diagnosis of possible attention deficit hyperactivity disorder (ADHD) as an explanation of his difficulties; she also requested help in managing home life. Charlie drew a happy face and a sad face to illustrate his view of himself in school, and reported he was bullied by other children. The desired outcomes were described as Charlie having better self-control, to be able to play without becoming aggressive, and to have more positive family relationships.

The panel accepted the request, and this was formally relayed to the school in question by letter; an educational psychologist was designated to be the key worker, and had overall co-ordinating responsibility for the case, monitoring practice and communicating regularly with the school and parents, as well as providing specific educational psychology provision. The panel also decided that family therapy support for the parents was desirable as part of the initial support, as little was understood about the needs of the family. The team felt it was important to unpick the reasons for the change in Charlie's behaviour in both home and school life.

Intervention

The educational psychologist's intervention began with a class observation followed by detailed discussion with Charlie's teacher: Charlie was one of a small group of children who were difficult to manage, but he was often the one most noticed because of his physical size. Over a period of six weeks a more effective learning environment was explored and devised, consisting of whole class rewards and sanctions; positive achievable targets for the group of 'controlling' children; and an individual mentoring plan for Charlie through sessions with a learning mentor based on raising his self-esteem, anger management and appropriate social skills. Charlie was also encouraged to help younger pupils in his class who were underachieving.

After the six-week period, the class teacher reported significant positive changes in both Charlie's behaviour and the class as a whole.

The family therapy intervention began with a meeting with the parents, who agreed a contract of work with the therapists. The family consisted of a young mum and dad, a sister a year older than Charlie, and a baby sister. The paternal grandmother was a strong presence in the family. The therapy began as couple work, examining their conflicting parental styles through understanding their own parenting experiences, and the role of heavy-handed discipline expected of fathers. The meaning of the mother-in-law's 'unhelpful' help was explored.

The therapy moved on to whole family work, based on structural and solution-focused methodology, involving miracle questions and preferred futures for each family member. Charlie felt 'unheard' in the middle of his family and anxious about the high expectations of being the only boy in the family and feeling he needed to act as a 'hard' man. At a panel review it was decided that Charlie would benefit from some individual therapeutic support with the dramatherapist so that his voice could be heard and his needs within the family understood. Through offering that secure safe place just for Charlie, he was able to share his innermost thoughts and gain confidence in talking to his parents. Charlie wanted to attend drama club, and his dad agreed to take him to it, although he had previously thought it was too 'soft'. Charlie's mum had suffered a miscarriage before the youngest child was born, and family loss and difficult emotional issues had not been discussed or explained appropriately. In a joint session with the dramatherapist, the family was supported in finding new ways of talking about these issues with Charlie. New house rules were established with the agreement of everyone, and Charlie was encouraged to do particular tasks by giving him choices in how he went about doing them.

Reviewing the therapeutic work with the family, everyone felt they were calmer and happier. However, Charlie still felt scared at break times and sometimes felt a desire to 'run out' from situations in school.

The flexibility and fluidity of the team allows other professionals to become involved as the case progresses, and the key worker is responsible for the overall review of the work involved.

Key worker role

The key worker in each case (in this instance the educational psychologist) is responsible for the overall view of the work, the progress of that work, and making sure that communication between the involved team members is appropriate and effective. The key worker represents the team and the case for the school, child and family, maintaining appropriate links with each one.

In this request the educational psychologists and drama and family therapists communicated regularly with each other, and after their respective interventions the case was reviewed at the next weekly team panel meeting. The work changed to include the youth intervention officer from the team, who spent time discussing with Charlie, through individual and class group work, about personal safety and incorporating strategies in how to deal with aspects of bullying. More appropriate ways of finding a safe place in school, rather than trying to run out, were devised, with school support. The family had recently begun to think about moving house, another cause of anxiety and tension in the home. The youth intervention officer's work evolved into transition support for Charlie, about moving house and the transition from Foundation to Key Stage One in school.

The key worker reviewed the case work with the BIP co-ordinator and the parents in school. Charlie was calmer in school, and his aggressive and disruptive behaviour was markedly reduced. The parents reported that home life was more relaxed and they were more confident in their combined parenting skills, resulting in a decrease in tension and anxieties for everyone. Both school and family now had a different view of Charlie, understanding that his difficult behaviour was a manifestation of anxieties and worries, belying a sensitive and ultimately kind boy. Charlie's mother's fears about Charlie 'having ADHD' were reduced. Charlie began engaging with his learning once more.

Exiting process

The needs-led ethos of the team and the ongoing assessments determine the time limits of each request; in other words, the work is *not* time-limited.

The exiting process for Charlie's case was initiated with a formal exiting letter sent to the school, with separate evaluation forms about the outcomes of the work filled in by the child, the parents or carers, and the BIP co-ordinator.

The outcomes of the request for involvement had been met: Charlie had better self-control, he was able to develop more appropriate ways of playing that didn't involve aggression, and more positive relationships in his family life were established. The panel formally exited the multi-agency team support with the school, with the proviso that if more interventions were required at a later date the school would be able to re-refer. The school, Charlie and his family filled in their evaluation forms: significant improvement was noted for attainment, risk of exclusion, and a reduction in anti-social behaviour; Charlie drew a happy face and described feeling less anxious and his family as 'cool'; and his family reported that 'everyone gets on better and we are more aware of everyone's needs: thanks for all the support'.

Special needs

If the work with Charlie had identified the need for additional specialist support, a referral to other agencies, such as CAMHS, would have been undertaken. ADHD is an example of a mental health anxiety disorder that may require a diagnosis and medication, for example. Special educational needs (SEN) refers to children who have learning difficulties or disabilities that make it harder for them to learn or access education than most children of similar age. Help is usually provided within the school setting through supportive programmes, but some children may require extra-specialist support from other agencies that have the necessary diagnostic support and health specialisms to meet specific needs.

During their contact work with children and their families, the team members in the multi-agency support team may have concerns about children's welfare. The Common Assessment Framework (CAF) programme has been developed in recent years to support professionals to make judgements about how to help children and families in the best interest for safeguarding the child. The framework allows for gaining an understanding of a child's developmental needs, the capacity of parents or carers to respond appropriately to those needs and keep them from harm, and to understand the environmental impact on home life (Safeguarding Children 2005).

All multi-agency teams and other agencies working with children are required by law to ensure that the risks to harm are minimized, and if necessary take action to address those concerns about neglect, abuse or the risk of criminal activity. Social care involvement may need to be activated, and the teams provide access to a range of support, working in partnership with parents, families and the local community.

All agencies and support services have a duty of care to protect children and young people from harm, and address any concerns for their safety. In the case of Charlie, there were no significant concerns about his welfare, and no further involvement from our team or other specific agencies was required at that time.

Evaluation

The work of this particular team service was studied as part of a PhD research project undertaken by S. Lippel (2006) to explore the factors involved in multi-agency working from the perspective of the professionals as well as service users. The research highlighted two common themes – identity and values – that had relevance to both the service users and deliverers. It was established that a multi-agency team, which is easily accessible and based within its local community, shares an understanding of the values of *that particular* community with its service users, and thus both benefit from each other. The overarching principles of therapy and psychology that informed this particular team service resulted in some 'homogeneity of practice' between team members, a transferring of knowledge, skills and competencies that was 'comprehensive and aligned' (Lippel 2006).

Families' previous experiences of some service providers had left them feeling that their identities were discounted or ignored. The systemic aspect of the team practice meant that the life histories of parents and children were heard and understood, strengthening an acceptance of their own sense of identity, which enabled changes to occur.

The research project revealed that values and beliefs were central to effective practice, cited by both service users and providers. Working with, and understanding, underlying values and respecting diversity 'prevents endorsing some values over others...allowing practitioners to be open, empathetic, trustworthy and genuinely interested' for their clients (Lippel 2006). Authenticity and genuineness were pre-requisites for team members, as was creativity and an openness to new ways of working in a shared culture that is overt and is effectively communicated to the people who access the service. Service team members learn from each other and from the parents and children with whom they work.

The flexibility of the professional role in the multi-agency support team is one of the key features of the extended school service, with its capacity-building aspect and wide range of work. The needs-led perspective, as opposed to time allocation service, is another defining feature of effective practice. Improvements in children's behaviour, concentration and motivation to learn, as well as an increased capacity to cope with difficulties, are reported in many of the outcomes of requests for involvement. The multi-agency team model, with practitioners seconded or recruited into the team, allows scope to engage in work at a range of levels, and team members maintain links with their home agencies or therapeutic registering bodies for supervision and practice training. The willingness to think 'multi-agency', with regular meetings to share information and ideas without preciousness about roles, is key to effectiveness (DfES 2004). The lack of hierarchy, with practitioners seeing themselves as part of a unified team working within the ethos of an holistic approach, was seen to be critical to the effectiveness of any team's work.

Impact of support

A sample evaluation of the overall BIP programme in the UK was carried out to assess the impact nationally of some of the BIP initiatives undertaken. The research (Hallam 2007) highlighted the following points:

- evidence of improved behaviour

- positive changes to school policies and practices

- positive changes to school ethos

- improved relationship with parents

- improvement in children's well-being and learning

- reduction in staff stress

- reduction in time spent managing poor behaviour.

Levels of attendance rose nationally, albeit by small amounts; however, the impact on pupils meant that they *wanted* to attend school, and their parents felt supported in persuading their children to attend. Impact of work with pupils, implemented by learning mentors, for example, focusing on anger management, self-esteem and transition, was successful in supporting children identified as being 'at risk'. One of the key findings of Hallam's research suggested that, in the various ways that the different BIPs functioned, the greatest overall improvements in attendance and attainment were achieved through the adoption of a multi-agency approach for the implementation of support.

As part of the national BIP initiative, the collaboration in the South West locality illustrates a multi-disciplinary team approach to multi-agency working. Children, parents and teachers have appreciated the availability of therapeutic input provided by counsellors and therapists, recognizing the support from practitioners who were not authoritative school figures.

Overall, the results of an evaluation of the schools in the collaboration that this multi-agency support team serviced showed that 90 per cent of schools reported improvement in attendance, 75 per cent reduction in exclusion and 78 per cent improvement in disaffection to learning. School BIP co-ordinators appreciated the input from the multi-agency team support for the direct work and also the therapeutic consultation provided to all school staff. Often professionals in schools who deal with mental health and psychological well-being are not necessarily therapeutically trained, and the multi-agency team's therapeutic model of consultation offered that reflective confidential support. The well-being of the school staff is as important as the well-being of the child.

Another important impact of this particular multi-agency support team service has been the critical incidence response. As well as supporting requests for involvement, the therapists, alongside the educational psychologists and other team members, have offered specialist support to individual children, schools and families following child protection issues, sudden deaths and other traumatic events.

The therapists from the team provided training for school staff, community-based generic training and specific training packages to other inter-agency workforces on emotional and behavioural issues such as attachment and bereavement, for example.

The team implemented a post-intervention evaluation of each request for involvement undertaken over the three-year period, obtaining the views of the school, parents or carers and the individual child in each of the referrals. The evaluation was based on the specific tangible outcomes for the child agreed at the outset, and other generic measures such as swift and easy access to support, knowledge and skills of the team, and an improved relationship between home and school.

Overall, the conclusions revealed that the tangible outcomes were 60 per cent fully met, 37 per cent satisfactorily met (acknowledging the need for ongoing support, possibly from other agencies) and 3 per cent not met. Qualitative comments from parents revealed the supportive impact of the team, such as 'We understand C's behaviour better now, and home life is much more relaxed', and 'Life is so much easier now'. Staff at school also had positive comments to make, such as 'This case (re H) has been really complex and ongoing, and being able to discuss different ways of exploring other avenues to manage it has been invaluable'. One child said 'I like you talking to my mum and dad' and another 'I'm not so sad any more'. All these comments demonstrate the positive impact of this particular multi-agency support team and multi-agency service.

WHAT ARE THE CHALLENGES?
Difficult challenges

As part of an extended school service, the referrals or requests for involvement to the multi-agency support team are, by definition, school based or educational, and indeed therapy work focus is initially perceived as such. Changes in perception and understanding of a school-based problem for a child, and a systemic ethos, allows for other contexts to be thought about and addressed.

Educational psychologists in some local authorities are sometimes required to fulfil statementing or statutory elements to their work in schools, rather than engage in collaborative practice in team work. This potential tension between the multi-agency team professional and their seconding agency may need delicate negotiation.

Systemic thinking and principles 'as a basis for thinking about problems is a relatively recent phenomenon' (Dowling and Osborne 2003, p.101). Some agencies who do not work to this ethos have difficulty in understanding the benefits of collaborative thinking, and that known tried and tested methods of working do not require change. A preoccupation with the individual is sometimes still prevalent in thinking about a problem for the child, and the most appropriate intervention should be addressed at that level. Resistance to change and letting go of assumptions and historical ways of working has proved problematical in the setting up of some multi-agency working.

'Behaviour' defined as good or bad is a hurdle for the understanding of any social and emotional difficulties, and school staff dealing with the pressures of inspections of every child's academic attainment have less time to maintain and think about the caregiving aspects of their role. Some primary schools have maintained a 'closed system' and found difficulties in joining with a collaborative 'open system' philosophy of a multi-agency approach to the school system. A different belief system can offer different interventions and other solutions to problems, but sometimes strong beliefs and attitudes are hard to change. Some of the local authorities set up 'in house' multi-agency teams that found it hard to maintain an objective and independent standpoint.

Other services or agencies that address health issues recognize the multi-agency teams as supporting the 'middle ground' and the early intervention level of support; such teams are seen to provide a 'bridge in' to more specialized agencies. Inappropriate referrals on the part of the school, or the acceptance of an inappropriate request for involvement by the team, sometimes occur, and are guarded against by ongoing supervision and training for school co-ordinators and team members. Complex health needs and medication, for example, are always the main concern and priority of the appropriate clinical health professionals.

The collaborative aspects of multi-agency work in teams means a blurring of the unique and distinctive contributions of each team member and may lead to an unrealistic or inappropriate level of expertise and possible dangerous practice. Any power differentials that occur between professionals, and the beliefs that some skills are 'better' than others, still exist in the workplace, and it is hoped the collaborative nature and ethos of multi-agency work will overcome these professional difficulties.

It is possible to be the victims of success, and capacity issues are relevant for the multi-agency team described here and other multi-agency teams nationally. Time-limitless interventions or open-ended work brings with it inherent problems. Professional boundaries in terms of capacity are addressed at team level through supervision, and time and commitment rather than a time-allocated model is a necessary requirement for successful multi-agency work; monitoring the effectiveness of time-limitless work allows for successful outcomes.

Exciting challenges

As therapists, our experience of working in a team has become second nature through reflective team practice. The multi-disciplinary approach meant that dramatherapists and creative art therapists extended their practice of working in schools, in one-to-one sessions, to include joint sessions and team working. The South West multi-agency team offered an innovative and exciting opportunity for therapists of different persuasions to work together, and be involved in a multi-agency team that was based on systemic thinking and principles.

All the members of this team were open to be challenged, as opposed to being conformist and resistant to change. The pervading systemic ethos of the team allowed for differing views and perspectives to work alongside each other, rather than being 'the right way' to do things. The specific principle of hypothesizing, inherent in systemic methodology, is enhanced by the theoretical framework of other team members' practice groundings. The team were encouraged to think of alternatives, to 'think the unthinkable', rather than falling back on an expert opinion. For some of the educational psychologists, the opportunity to work closely with therapists was an exciting challenge that offered a way for innovative practice and recognition of the significance of therapeutic interventions.

The ideas and examples illustrated in the pioneering approach depicted in the seminal text by Dowling and Osborne (1994) provided the framework for subsequent multi-agency teams that followed in the ensuing years. Many of the clinical and educational psychologists who were part of that pioneering approach were trained at the Tavistock Clinic, a mental health service for children and families that was developed using innovative psychotherapy and a multi-disciplinary approach.

Therapy in schools is another exciting challenge: a different approach to dealing with difficulties and issues for children was beginning at this time to become thought of as 'mainstream' rather than something that happened in 'clinics'. This multi-agency support team in the South West was unique in incorporating different therapies and therapists as integral to the multi-agency approach to supporting children and their families, and schools. The evidence-based success of this multi-agency support team initiative that supported therapy, joint working and systemic philosophy illustrates an exciting model of multi-agency working.

JOINT WORKING

Ye cannot live for yourselves; a thousand fibres connect you
with your fellow-men.
[Henry Melvill]

DRAMATHERAPY AND FAMILY THERAPY IN PRACTICE

Having explored the history, discipline and application of dramatherapy, family therapy and multi-agency working, this piece will endeavour to explain how they may come together in one practice. We will look at the methodology, techniques and principles that dramatherapy and family therapy have in common before considering how they may extend and support each other in a multi-agency setup. A brief history of one such partnership will be given, along with examples of its application, and authentic case studies describing some of the various issues handled will be included throughout the piece to clarify the points raised.

Commonalities

Perhaps the most important reason why dramatherapy and family therapy produce such a harmonious and effective working relationship is that they have in common some baseline principles.

The first of these must be that both disciplines describe their approach as 'non-expert'. Dramatherapy talks about 'being' with the client (in this case the child) and entering his world, allowing him to direct proceedings until such time as the therapist deems it appropriate to move the process on by suggesting alternative material. The family therapist adopts the stance of 'not knowing' and comes from a position of curiosity about the family with whom they are meeting. Both therapies are content to explore their client's world for however long it takes to find out how it is rather than jumping to preconceived notions of how it might be.

In addition to starting from where the client is, both interventions lay tremendous importance on, and are prepared to invest an enormous amount of time in, forming a relationship of mutual trust: the therapeutic relationship in dramatherapy and the therapeutic alliance in family therapy. It can be seen, therefore, how, on the whole, the joint working practice of a drama and family therapist may consensually allow clients to bring their own material for assessment and therapy for some time before directive interventions are suggested.

The directive interventions or techniques themselves are often very similar in nature and focus. Amanda Strevitt Smith, in her interesting article on 'Dramatherapy with the Context of Systemic Family Therapy', says that 'systemic family therapy, like dramatherapy, focuses on the relationships, stories and narratives told and heard and the metaphorical use of language' (Strevitt Smith 2010).

CASE STUDY:
GEMMA – DEPRESSION

Background

Staff at school had been concerned about eight-year-old Gemma for a long time. Her family background was chaotic to say the least, with underage pregnancies and trouble with the police being just two of the issues relating to her older siblings. Her mother had struggled for a long time to bring up her large family, with only intermittent help from her husband, who seemed to come and go from the family home. However, when he was there he appeared to be a force to be reckoned with, and all the children seemed scared of his temper and tactics. Alcohol abuse was a problem in the family, and was finally the main cause of the father's premature death at the age of 40.

For a while after her father died Gemma's behaviour surprisingly improved. She stopped being so aggressive and bullying with her classmates and seemed quieter and calmer. Gradually, though, this quietness became, in itself, a cause for concern as Gemma became more and more withdrawn. Staff described her as seeming lifeless, with no light in her eyes. When asked to choose an activity, she usually shrugged and said she 'didn't care'. The only time she showed any interest in anything was, apparently, if she was playing a particular board game which centred on a game of chance.

Naturally enough, her schoolwork was suffering. Gemma had never been a high achiever but had managed to hold her own with her peer group. Now she was slipping more and more behind, which, in turn, had a detrimental effect on her self-esteem. The tangible outcomes were for Gemma to re-immerse herself in her schoolwork and for her to take an interest in her surroundings again. In short, even at eight years old, it was felt that Gemma was suffering from depression.

Intervention

Initially the case was taken on by the family therapist on the team who worked with the family on issues of bereavement. The family needed a great amount of support since the eldest daughter had just had a baby son who was under the Court of Protection because of the drug-induced violence of his father. The second daughter had just announced that she too was pregnant again, which, when the baby was born, would make eight people living in a small terraced house. The family therapist decided that, until the family was more stable, there was very little point on trying to have any therapeutic input, and the case was referred back to social services. The case was kept open with multi-agency support, however, since the team's police liaison officer was continuing to work with the older boys and I, as the dramatherapist on the team, had begun to work with Gemma in school.

Although the family therapist had come to the conclusion that the family would not be able to benefit from therapeutic work at this stage, it was felt by the whole multi-agency support team that it was a different matter for Gemma. Under normal circumstances, if a child is not in a safe place, or abuse is ongoing, then my practice as a dramatherapist has always been that this situation would need to be addressed first before any therapeutic input could or would be effective. Having said this, there have been circumstances where I have supported a child in a non-therapeutic way while the background situation was being sorted. This, I felt, was one of these situations: I could begin to support Gemma in a non-directive way while other authorities worked to bring her family life under control. The family therapists would then, it was hoped, be able to resume their intervention as well.

My initial session with Gemma left me feeling lifeless: an interesting observation considering this was how she appeared to others. She chose a lion to represent herself, saying that this was her favourite animal. Unfortunately the lion could not stand up alone and had to have the support of another lion. This was as far as projective work with Gemma went. She did not want to tell any stories or play with the puppets; she said she could not draw or paint, and for the first few sessions all she wanted to do was to play her favourite board game: one in which everything was down to luck and no skills seemed to be involved whatsoever.

I wondered what Gemma was trying to tell us through her fascination with this specific game and, using the metaphor of the game, we gradually began to discuss life in general (and the raw and unexpected deals it sometimes delivered) and then Gemma's life in particular. I learnt that Gemma felt trapped in her tiny house with all these chaotic people around her, so much so that she often felt like jumping out of the window and running away. When her father was home, although she was scared of his volatile temper, he had brought a semblance of order to the house and some sort of structure to family life. Whenever things seemed to be going a little better, something would happen to take this 'improvement' away.

Now that her father was dead, there seemed to be no respite from 'things going wrong': the latest being that she had been told her beloved pet cat would have to be put down because of the imminent arrival of her sister's baby. If something is continually taken away from you, you learn not to care about it, and this, I felt, was what had happened to Gemma. She felt she had no choice in any matter and that everything was down to luck – usually bad luck.

I decided to go back to doing some embodiment work with Gemma to take her out of her mind with its negative thoughts and into her body. We started using clay, and after a couple of sessions in which Gemma just made unrecognizable shapes and said she was 'no good at this', she finally announced that she would like to make a bird. While moulding and remoulding the clay, Gemma told me about how she used to help her father feed the birds that he kept in a shed at the bottom of the garden. It was her special time: the only time she could remember having with him, and she said that he had been a different person, much gentler and kinder, when handling his birds.

Outcomes

During the weeks that it took to make Gemma's bird, events had moved on at home and provision had been made for the eldest daughter and her family to be re-housed. The police involvement with the two lads was also having some effect, and family life as a whole appeared calmer and more structured. The family therapist assessed the family as being in a better place to receive therapeutic support, and sessions had begun with the whole family. The family therapy sessions involved Gemma, her mother and the boys playing board games that focused on each member of the family, and their thoughts and feelings about each other. There had never been any time for any fun or good times together. Family life had been reactive and frightening for Gemma. Building on the somewhat calmer and more structured family life, which was certainly less chaotic, Gemma was able to feel more held and supported within her family.

Gemma was beginning to come back to life. We had painted her bird, and she proudly took it to show her friends in class. Then she announced that she wanted to make a cage for it 'so that it could get a bit of peace', which we duly did out of a cardboard box and cane sticks. Painted and varnished and with a makeshift perch for the bird, it all began to look quite lifelike. In her penultimate sessions I asked Gemma if we needed to lock the door of the cage so that the bird wouldn't fly away. 'Oh no,' she replied. 'We can leave it open – the bird knows it can go whenever it wants to, so it doesn't want to now. It's happy to stay in its cage.'

Through their use of metaphorical language, both drama and family therapy employ dramatic distancing to give their clients the opportunity to view their problems objectively rather than becoming embroiled in an emotional subjectivity. Incidentally, the metaphorical language that a child or family uses is often very revealing, as in the 'right as rain', 'mortal combat' and 'survival' terms referred to in the section 'Metaphor' on p.73. As described in the case study of Gemma, the drama or family therapist will often consciously look for a metaphor to describe a situation that can then be exploited using creative methods.

Dramatic distancing, as previously described and referenced, is applied in both disciplines through techniques using both role and projected images. Strevitt Smith draws parallels between the projection method of dramatherapy, where the therapist uses small figures, toys or puppets to encourage the child to externalize his feelings, and the narrative approach of family therapy that externalizes the problem in the family, often giving it an interactive form (Strevitt Smith 2010).

Humour is most certainly an important tool in helping the child and family view their problems as solvable and not momentous. Just as a dramatherapist might give a name to that naughty little demon which sneaks up on a child and makes him lose his temper, so a family therapist might involve the family in looking humorously at their externalized problem. In this way the emphasis in both scenarios is on the dissolution of the problem rather than giving it greater weight through analysis.

Thus the difficulty for the child or the family is not seen as an integral and therefore unsolvable part of themselves but rather as something which can be faced and, often using humour or creative interventions, overcome. A delightful example of this is the well-documented case of 'Mr Sneaky Poo', who sneaks up on the child and causes him to soil his pants, and thus has to be outwitted by the combined efforts of therapist and child. Using this method, the problem is seen as something to be overcome in a playful way rather than something awful for which the child is to blame.

Playfulness is also an approach used by both disciplines to great effect. In encouraging the family to hypothesize, sometimes wildly, about a situation, the family therapist introduces an element of fun into the proceedings and lightens an atmosphere that has hitherto been heavy with the 'weight of the problem'. Playful fun is at the centre of nearly every dramatherapy session, and unites dramatherapist and child in the same way that it unites members of the family in a family therapy session.

CASE STUDY:
SOFIA – LEARNT BEHAVIOUR

Background

When Sofia was referred to the multi-agency support team she was six years old and had been in England for the last two. Her family had moved from the Czech Republic after a series of upheavals, which had necessitated them living in the North of England for a while. Mum had split up from Sofia's dad while in Manchester but was now living with her new partner, the father of Sofia's baby brother. Staff at school said that, despite all their efforts, Sofia continued to be disruptive in class, refusing to sit still or listen, and displaying very aggressive behaviour towards her peer group. At home Mum was at her wits' end about Sofia as she was constantly arguing and becoming uncooperative and angry if things didn't go her way. Mum complained that, although Sofia would never do what her mother said, she obeyed her partner at the first time of asking.

Both school and home had tried various strategies to little or no effect. Sticker charts worked for a while, as did time out and rewards for good behaviour. Privileges taken away only resulted in Sofia reiterating that she 'didn't understand', 'couldn't do it' and was a very 'bad girl', whereupon she behaved so morosely that staff were beginning to wonder if she was suffering from depression.

The language barrier might have been a possible reason for the behaviour except that, although Sofia spoke no English when she arrived in England, her command of the language was now excellent and there was no doubt that Sofia understood everything that was going on.

The tangible outcomes focused on Sofia being able to work effectively in a group, on her building up good relationships with her peer group, and the family understanding and developing strategies to cope with her behaviour.

Intervention

It was decided that the intervention in Sofia's case would involve four different team members: a family therapist would support the family in the home, an educational psychologist would do a class visit to assess whether Sofia had any learning needs, a learning support mentor would do some group work with Sofia based on communication and social skills, and, as key worker and dramatherapist, I would conduct a number of sessions with Sofia to try to discover what was really troubling her.

The report came back from the educational psychologist to the effect that Sofia was a bright, intelligent girl who was functioning at slightly above average for her age and had no trouble completing her work, when she wanted to.

This last was the crux of the matter. There appeared to be something that prevented Sofia from wanting to perform and behave well. Was it worry, low self-esteem, friendship problems or sheer laziness?

After a couple of dramatherapy sessions it became apparent that friendship issues featured very highly in Sofia's life. The group sessions with the learning mentor were going well and appeared to be having some effect, in that meal-time assistants reported that Sofia was no longer sitting by herself in the playground. In spite of this, Sofia continued to tell me, in a very sad voice, that she 'had no friends at all'. In fact, many of Sofia's stories seemed to centre on a very lonely elephant which also had 'no friends at all'. At home Mum reported the same sort of behaviour. If chastised, Sofia would sit for hours in such a state of gloom that, as her mum admitted, she would often take pity on her and rescind the punishment.

After some visits the family therapist was able to report that she was working with Mum in particular on discipline issues. Mum's boyfriend had no trouble with Sofia, and it was obvious that they had an exceedingly good relationship, although Sofia was inclined to appeal to her mother if she did not want to do what Stefan said. The situation was beginning to cause a rift in the parents' relationship. With gentle encouragement, Mum was able to explain to the family therapist the reasons why she always found it difficult to maintain a level of discipline with Sofia. The disruption and trauma that she and Sofia had experienced in the early days of Sofia's life had resulted in Mum always feeling that she had, somehow, to 'make it up' to Sofia. Sofia had learnt from an early age that, in order to get what she wanted, she had only to put on a very sad face and Mum would, at once, begin to feel guilty. She had tried to continue this victim strategy at school and found that it did not work.

While the family therapist continued to work with Mum on her issues of guilt, I worked with Sofia, first on helping her to compartmentalize the events of her early childhood, and then looking at her problems of motivation. To counteract her habitual use of the sad 'victim' mode, I used humour in the form of a fictitious character called Miss Moanie, who would sneak up on Sofia and turn down the corners of her face when she was least expecting it. Together with the educational psychologist and Sofia's teacher, we also devised a system of short-term goals and rewards which would help Sofia examine the consequences of positive versus negative behaviour.

Outcomes

After some weeks the school reported that the first two tangible outcomes had been met, in that Sofia, as a naturally lively and charismatic child, was usually a ringleader in the playground and that, on the whole, she was much better at working in a group in class, although there too she liked to be the centre of attention. Mum was finding it easier to manage Sofia at home where, with Stefan's support, she was beginning to see Sofia's 'victim' role for what it was and joined with him in playfully teasing Miss Moanie away. The behaviour which had served Sofia well for so long was now outdated but, as with all learnt behaviours, would take time to 'unlearn'.

It may be said that both dramatherapy and family therapy use a systems approach in their application of role-play. Whereas dramatherapy concentrates on helping the client explore the roles they play and on developing different ones which possibly might serve them better in their general interaction with the outside world, family therapy endeavours to encourage the family to find new and creative ways of looking at the roles they play within the family system.

Thus similarities may be drawn between the 'closed' family system, which finds itself unable to adapt to elements outside its own system, and the individual who finds himself trapped in a dysfunctional way of being, unable to find the flexibility to play a more functional role.

To do this, both therapies employ techniques taken from dramatherapy and psychodrama such as reflecting, sculpting, mirroring, doubling, role reversal and reframing. The reflecting team, which in family therapy comments upon the situation a family brings, thereby allowing the family to view their personal problems through an objective lens, is reminiscent of the Playback theatre of dramatherapy which uses performance to externalize and objectify the client's story for him.

Using sculpts in therapy, a family may be encouraged to arrange themselves into a scene with body language that shows the problem at the moment and then again how it would be if the problem were solved. In dramatherapy a child will use body positions to show the therapist how he is feeling and how it would be if he were to feel better. In both interventions the therapists may mirror, speak or act for a child, members of the family or projected image, thereby allowing their clients a deeper insight into the situation presented.

Role reversal, used in the same way, is a powerful tool for gaining empathy and understanding of how other members of the family or significant others in a child's life may be feeling. Similarly, reframing techniques introduce a fresh and infinitely more positive perspective to a hitherto entrenched, introspective and negative belief system. A 'show, don't tell' philosophy, usually being the preferred way of working in both approaches, may therefore be said to be another of the baseline principles which drama and family therapy have in common.

CASE STUDY:
JESSICA – ACUTE ANXIETY

Background

Jessica, aged seven, was referred to the multi-agency support team with concerns that she was becoming school phobic. Both Mum and school were very concerned as to how anxious Jessica had become of late, not wanting to leave Mum in the morning, and often saying she had a tummy ache and wanted to go home during the day. Her attendance level had dropped dramatically over the last term, and Mum felt that something was bothering her, although she didn't know what. Even Jessica said she didn't know why she felt anxious about coming to school when hither-to she had not. Whatever it was, her younger sister did not seem to be affected by it and continued to attend school regularly and happily. Jessica's dad had left home two years previously and Mum had a new boyfriend who was now living with them.

The tangible outcomes stated that everyone would like to see Jessica coming to school in the mornings without any upset, that the root of her anxieties be discovered and that Mum could feel reassured that Jessica was not holding any big worries.

Intervention

In a case such as this it is clearly paramount to meet with all parties concerned and to do as much information gathering as possible in order to address potential child protection issues. A family therapist and dramatherapist met with the headteacher, class teacher, Mum and new boyfriend to try to put together a sequence of events and establish the trigger point for Jessica's behaviour. Although numerous phone calls were made to Dad's mobile, he remained unavailable. Both Mum and her boyfriend assured the meeting that relationships at home were good but that Jessica refused to sleep in her own room at night and had to have her bed brought into Mum and boyfriend's room. Her sister continued to be unaffected by all this and to sleep in the room vacated by Jessica. Mum's concerns centred on the fact that, although Dad had contact with Jessica and her sister, he was often unreliable and let the girls down. It was obvious that the relationship between Mum and Dad was not amicable and that Mum thought that the number of times that Jessica had been let down by Dad might have been having an effect on her.

Jessica's statement that she liked school and wasn't having any problems there was confirmed by her teacher and by the team's educational psychologist, who did a class and playground observation. While my family therapist colleague continued to meet with Mum and boyfriend at home, I began dramatherapy sessions with Jessica on a weekly basis.

Jessica loved the sessions and very quickly opened up to talk about her feelings through puppets. It became obvious that she was very happy at home, loved her mum and had a good relationship with the boyfriend. She wished she could see more of her dad and felt let down when he did not arrive to take her and her sister out, but not overly so since her mum and boyfriend always took them somewhere else 'nice' instead. Sometimes even better, because often 'all we do is watch telly at Dad's'.

The situation remained a mystery. The family therapist reported that there seemed to be no obvious cause for concern at home. Sessions with Jessica continued with her playing happily with the puppets. It was obvious that Jessica was a very intelligent, sensitive and imaginative child, a fact that was confirmed by her class teacher. After a couple of weeks the nature of Jessica's stories changed. They suddenly became excessively violent, with people stealing children away and threatening each other with knives. With Jessica's permission I discussed this with the family therapist, and we queried whether Jessica had witnessed such violence either within the family home or in the neighbourhood. The information we received made this an unlikely answer.

Meanwhile school reported that Jessica seemed a little happier about leaving Mum in the mornings, but we felt we still hadn't got to the root of the problem.

A recurrent theme, however, seemed to be emerging in Jessica's stories: two princesses being killed by their sisters who were watching over them from afar. The girls never knew when they were going to be attacked since these sisters hid in cupboards and under beds. They seemed to be the princesses' own evil counterparts, although Jessica never called them that. The story smacked of psychological horror and was totally different to Jessica's previous work, as was Jessica's demeanour and level of energy. When I asked her where this story had come from, she replied that it reminded her of a film she had seen at her dad's house some time ago.

We played through the story again and again, first using projection and then in role, and finally I asked Jessica how she would like to change the ending.

We played through her ideas a couple of times. Jessica seemed very energized until at last she announced that she had 'done that story and wanted to do another'.

Outcomes

The first tangible outcome was met, in that now Jessica was leaving Mum in the mornings with no trouble. In a meeting at home with Mum, boyfriend, the family therapist and myself, we cautiously, without attributing blame, discussed the possible cause of Jessica's anxiety. It was apparent that Jessica had been deeply affected by this film (which her sister had not seen) and had somehow identified with one of the princesses. Subconsciously she felt her life was constantly in danger from some unknown entity that could attack her at any time unless she was with her mother. The fact that her mother had fairly recently taken on a new partner, although she liked him, would have also made her feel less safe. It was felt that Jessica was an example of a highly sensitive child being deeply affected by witnessed material that her conscious mind could not understand and which had therefore been deeply rooted in her subconscious where it had continued to bombard her with feelings of acute and incomprehensible anxiety. Jessica had been unable to 'tell' anyone what was wrong. It was only through her subconsciously motivated play that she was eventually able to 'show' me.

Jessica returned to the sessions after Christmas in a high state of excitement. As a reward for sleeping in her own room throughout the holidays, she was allowed to go on holiday to Butlin's with her friend's family. This was for a whole week – and without her mum!

Not only do the two therapies have many intervention techniques in common, they also tend to be regarded as most useful for similar life issues. Just as strategic family therapy acknowledges as difficult, and works with, the transitional stages in family life, so dramatherapy is often used to incorporate and assimilate transitional phases – for example, house or school moves – within the life of the child.

CASE STUDY: CHELLAM – MULTI-CULTURAL ISSUES

Background

Chellam was referred to the multi-agency support team over concerns about her state of mental health since she had tried to set herself on fire. An articulate and intelligent ten-year-old, Chellam had been living in England with her family – mother, father and three young sisters – for the last four years. The family members had fled the troubles in their own country and were now living under the threat of extradition. The incident that led to Chellam threatening suicide was the turning down of an appeal for asylum.

As a result of having witnessed atrocities in her own country, Chellam's mother was suffering from clinical depression and found it difficult to care for her children. Chellam often found herself in the position of carer, not only for her mother but also for her two younger sisters. Social services were already involved with the family since there had been some incidences of domestic violence in the past and concerns over her mother's state of mental health.

The crux of the problem appeared to be cultural since, living as it were under the constant threat of extradition, the family was falling apart, with the father drinking heavily and the mother becoming more and more depressed and unable to manage her increasingly badly behaved younger daughters. In addition, there was the cultural belief that suicide was an acceptable exit strategy if things became too bad, and this was openly talked about in the home.

The tangible outcomes for Chellam centred on an assessment of her mental health needs, with appropriate support being given as soon as possible. To this end a referral had been made to CAMHS, but the school felt that some support was needed in the interim.

Intervention

In an initial session with Chellam it became apparent that she was feeling under pressure from all sides. The worry of her mother's illness, having to be a carer for her small, difficult sisters, the threat of extradition and being confined in a small flat were all serving to increase Chellam's sense of frustration and helplessness. A naturally lively and intelligent girl, Chellam obviously needed outlets for her emotions and access to as many activities as possible to challenge, stimulate and take her mind away from the family's problems.

It was decided at the panel meeting that weekly dramatherapy sessions would enable Chellam to externalize her feelings. Additionally, a family therapist would work with Mum, and Dad if he were available. The main cause of the family's difficulties, namely the asylum application, was outside the remit of the team, but it was obvious that the whole family needed as much support as possible while a further application was being processed.

As Chellam was a year-six pupil and due to transfer to secondary school the following September, the educational welfare officer on the team researched the possibility of Chellam joining in some of the year-seven activities ahead of time, in particular the drama group, since, following the dramatherapy sessions, Chellam had expressed an interest in this. Transport was a problem for the family, so it was arranged that Chellam would be picked up twice a week after school to attend drama and dance classes at her prospective community college.

Provision was also made through the team for behaviour support to be given to the two younger siblings and, for the pre-school child, for Mum to access a suitable crèche, where she could also meet other parents from different cultures. Initially, Mum was very reluctant to do this, because of cultural differences, but when a suggestion was made for a family worker to accompany her, she cautiously agreed.

Meanwhile, drama and family therapy sessions, to enable Mum and Chellam to understand their feelings and come to terms with their situation, were continuing. Initial individual dramatherapy sessions soon gave way to joint sessions with Chellam's best friend, a Palestinian girl called Mari. Together, through stories and plays they invented themselves, Chellam and Mari explored what it was like to come from another country and how, deep down, they felt they did not really 'belong'.

At home the family therapist used a similar narrative technique to encourage Mum to share her feelings about swopping her own sense of 'belonging' for the relative safety of a country quite foreign to her. Unfortunately, Dad was not available to join in the sessions.

Outcomes

After some weeks of joint dramatherapy sessions, Chellam announced that she was feeling a lot happier. She absolutely loved the drama and dance activities, which not only provided an outlet for her creativity and physicality but also gave her respite from family life. She said her mum seemed a bit happier and her three little sisters weren't such 'pains' or perhaps she 'just felt better able to cope' with them. The dramatherapy sessions had taught her that she was not alone, and she and Mari were considering producing a play for their class or even the school about how it felt to come to a strange country.

With much gentle encouragement Mum had been able to confide in the family therapist and work through some of her issues, which centred on bereavement and post-traumatic stress. At Chellam's request, Dad was finally persuaded to attend some of the family sessions that were held with both the drama and family therapist. These sessions were essentially celebratory in nature and served to cement the progress that all members of the family had made.

In one of these sessions the family as a whole were able to look at cultural demands and differences, as well as the unsettling aspects of the transition from their native country. They were then able to share their experiences with one another, which helped them all understand the strain that each, in their own way, had been feeling. This increased the sense of togetherness that had been lacking and helped to externalize the problem of possible extradition rather than allowing it to become an integral part of the family.

Interestingly, as soon as the family had made moves towards an acceptance of the situation, they heard from the Home Office that their latest appeal for asylum had been granted!

However, perhaps the most important baseline principle integral to both drama and family therapy is the emphasis on the strengths of the individuals concerned. Both build on what is right about a situation rather than what is wrong. In dramatherapy the child is encouraged to find the 'hero' within himself; in family therapy the family are invited to answer the 'miracle question' of what would be different if everything were all right again. Neither therapy views the child as the problem, seeking instead to externalize the behaviour and set it against a background of extenuating circumstances.

In essence, it is the belief in the innate capability of both child and family member, given the appropriate platform and encouragement, to find within themselves the potential necessary for healing that underpins and makes effective the joint working relationship of a drama and family therapist.

CASE STUDY:
DANIEL – STEPFAMILIES

Background

Nine-year-old Daniel was referred to the multi-agency support team over the escalation in his aggressive, confrontational behaviour. The increased levels in disrespect and disobedience had recently led to a major incident which, in turn, had put Daniel at risk of exclusion. Staff said that Daniel was one of two boys who took it in turns to be the ringleaders, inciting other children to behave disruptively.

Daniel lived with his mum, two younger stepsisters and his dad, who he had just recently learnt was not his biological father. Daniel had, apparently, taken the news very badly and was extremely sensitive to any comments about his stepfather, reacting violently if teased. The family lived in a close-knit neighbourhood, and it was thought that this was not an easy situation for Daniel either, since there was much talk which Daniel had a habit of overhearing.

Mum said that she was finding it increasingly difficult to control Daniel at home, and he had started to be rude and defiant to his stepfather whom he seemed previously to adore.

Although Mum stated that Daniel had been difficult ever since he had been in the Foundation Class, the school was of the opinion that, until the start of this year, he had been a model pupil. Teachers and class assistants were genuinely sad about what they saw as a 'lovely boy going rapidly downhill' and spoke extensively about how they remembered Daniel being a class leader. Fundamentally, the headteacher was worried that Daniel would ultimately do something outrageous, which would leave him with no choice but to expel him.

The tangible outcomes asked that Daniel be given support in school to help him manage his behaviour so that there was a reduction in confrontations with staff, disruptive incidences and inciting others to disrespect and aggression. Additionally, support was required for Mum to help her understand what was upsetting Daniel and to find ways to manage him in the home.

Intervention

Since the focus of the work seemed to be the need to find out what was troubling Daniel to make him change his behaviour so radically, I, as dramatherapist, became the key worker on the case with a view to conducting a series of assessment sessions. My family therapy colleague arranged to visit Mum and Dad in the home to find out exactly what sort of support they felt they needed. In addition the team's educational psychologist organized a visit to the school to observe Daniel in the playground and, if appropriate, to offer any suggestions as to how to avoid these confrontational situations.

Daniel was eager to engage with the dramatherapy work from the very first session and, through the medium of puppets, talked openly of how he didn't much like the way he was behaving and would much rather return to the person he used to be. His favourite film was *Superman* and we discussed what it must feel like to be a leader. We made masks and enacted various scenes from the film, with Daniel playing the role of Superman himself. After some sessions and through deroling and retaining or discarding certain characteristics, Daniel was able to identify the feeling he had when inciting others to bad behaviour in the playground as being similar to the feeling of power he had when playing Superman.

A bright and intelligent boy, Daniel was able to process the fact that this same feeling of power could still be achieved but without the ultimately disastrous results he had been having. We discussed ways in which he could still be a leader but in a positive way, and Daniel made various suggestions. The support of his teacher and classroom assistant was enlisted, and Daniel made a concerted effort to exchange one friendship group for another.

In this he received additional help from the team's educational psychologist, who made certain suggestions to the school as to how playtime routines and supervision could be improved.

While Daniel was receiving support in school, the parents were visited by my family therapy colleague at home. The family therapy work centred on gaining an understanding of the family dynamics and the context of the close family members in the local neighbourhood. Both Mum and stepdad came from very strong family ties, and these were very influential in the way that Daniel's family unit related to each other. Through several sessions both Mum and stepdad were able to understand their own strong family stories and 'myths', as well as their ideas about family bonds and identities. The therapeutic work involved unpicking what being 'a dad' meant, biological or otherwise. The work progressed to supporting both parents in the way that they talked about difficult things to Daniel, so that they were able to relate to his shock about his own identity and sense of self. Both parents were able to accommodate and manage Daniel's displays of 'power' and headstrong behaviour in a better way, lessening the tension at home.

Outcomes

Once Daniel had decided he wanted to return to a more positive mode of behaviour, the change was immediate. Daniel had always been a headstrong boy and, having made up his mind to do something, he let very little stand in his way. Fortunately, this time the results were positive, and school were very pleased with him. This was reported back to home and, for a while, life there settled down, as Daniel's mum was able to praise Daniel for his improved attitude, which reflected in their relationship.

Unfortunately, just as the team was considering exiting the case, the stepfather's daughter died. Although Daniel had never been close to his stepsister, as she was some years older than him, he felt the family's grief keenly and reacted by shutting himself in his room for hours on end. During this time Daniel slipped back a little into his prior behaviour at school, but the increased support and understanding of the staff managed to divert any truly disastrous outcomes. After some weeks it was decided that my family therapist colleague and I would offer to visit the family together with a view to engaging the whole family in some bereavement work.

On the first visit Daniel refused to come down from his room, and it was only on a second visit when I brought in the masks we had made together that he ventured out to show his family what he had produced. Through the masks we were able to talk about feelings and include the stepfather, who still felt the loss of his daughter very strongly. In this, Daniel identified with the loss he felt over the father he had never known, and some reparation was made to the rift between him and his stepfather.

Thus it was that by identifying and assimilating what was 'strong' about themselves – Daniel's leadership skills and the strong bonds of the family members – the family as a whole was able to bring about its own restorative process.

On the last visit we left Daniel and his stepfather planning a visit to an away game for Arsenal.

A history of one joint working practice

Written from Penny's experience and perspective, this section will focus on the history of one such joint working, not so much as an example of best practice but more in an attempt to explain the needs underpinning the organic development of such a professional relationship or, in plainer terms, the way one thing grew out of the other!

AN EXPERIMENT WITH THERAPY

As a dramatherapist working in primary and secondary schools within an inner city setting, I was often amazed at the resilience and fortitude of the children who crossed my path. It was, as I said, 'not how badly behaved they were that interested me but how well they coped given the scope and depth of their problems' (McFarlane 2005 p.ix). At that time dramatherapy was a relatively new phenomenon within education and, in my area, was regarded as a pioneering experiment into the effectiveness of early psychodynamic intervention with children at risk of exclusion. Although the 'experiment' went well and we were able to extend the project to commission art and dramatherapists in over 25 schools across the city, I always had the sense that, working in isolation, I was privy to only one piece of the jigsaw and not the whole picture.

Although I had few doubts as to the efficacy of drama (or art) therapy in listening to, acknowledging and acting upon the lone voice of the child, there was a need to set that voice against the background of where it belonged. Practically, there was a sense of frustration on a Monday morning following a half-term holiday when the child with whom I had worked so hard, and who was showing such signs of improvement two weeks ago, had slipped right back into his old patterns of behaviour. Something else needed to change, and that something was beyond my control.

I started seeing parents with the child's permission, and together we worked out contracts, set targets and looked at ways in which relationships could be improved. Occasionally I ran play and dramatherapy sessions for the parent (usually mother) and child. I found, on the whole, this form of intervention achieved the desired results more quickly and more sustainably than working on an individual basis. There was often, however, still a piece missing in the form of the absent parent or carer who, like the elephant in the room, usually filled the space with their 'non-presence'.

Although this scenario is still very often the case even with joint working, the practice of working within a multi-agency team gave me the much sought-after opportunity to address some of the missing pieces of the jigsaw.

CASE STUDY:
PETER – BEREAVEMENT

Background

Peter was a very cherished but angry boy, who sometimes came to school spitting at his classmates, lashing out, head butting and throwing major tantrums. He acted out at home too in an aggressive manner, but at other times was a loveable, sweet little boy. Peter, who was five years old, had not only lost his mum but also his younger sister, who had both been tragically killed in a car accident two years previously.

He was being brought up by his father and paternal grandparents, living together in a close family unit. His father worked away from home for long periods, and the main extent of everyday parenting was provided by the grandparents. The grandparents had met with the SENCO to ask for help, and it seemed that up until now they had not wanted, nor felt they needed, any bereavement support. The school also wanted to feel more confident in implementing appropriate strategies to deal with Peter's anger.

The tangible outcomes requested that the school understood the different needs of bereaved children; that the grandparents be supported and reassured in managing Peter's aggression; and that Peter be able to understand his feelings and enjoy a more positive time at school.

Intervention

The multi-agency support panel decided that I, as a family therapist, and my dramatherapist colleague should have joint key worker roles because of our past experiences as bereavement therapists.

We initiated inset training for the school staff, both to help them understand the 'stages' of grief as well as the impact of bereavement on the cognitive and emotional development of children. The staff were concerned that the firm and consistent boundaries that were in place to deal with Peter's outbursts at school were appropriate: they needed to feel confident that providing the essential 'normality' of the school day was not only necessary but also entirely in Peter's interests, to ensure that the sad and troubled little boy felt secure when his world had so recently been turned upside down.

Both my dramatherapy colleague and I met with the grandparents, and heard their story of the death of their daughter-in-law and their granddaughter. The enormity of their loss had prevented them from accessing any previous support: the grandmother stating that she was afraid to cry and 'let go' in case she could never stop. They found the responses of other family members difficult, in that other people avoided any mention of the deaths and were also avoiding the grandparents altogether, adding to their feeling of isolation. Their relief in being able to 'mention the unmentionable' was palpable.

The grandparents struggled with providing parenting boundaries, on the one hand as elderly people with a lively boy, and on the other because they felt it was not their rightful place when Peter still had a father, albeit absent from day-to-day life. Identities and roles play an important part in how we see ourselves, and taking on different roles and 'stepping into the breach' involved very mixed feelings for them.

The next phase of the therapeutic support involved several sessions with the grandparents and Peter together at home for joint family bereavement work such as drawing a family tree or genogram which depicted Peter's mother and baby sister in the centre of the family. Young children often fear the special person who has died will be forgotten altogether. By talking about their special people at every opportunity, we helped the recovery process take place; the protective avoidance of mentioning someone generally creates more problems in the future.

In further sessions we helped the family create memory boxes and also salt sculptures, each one depicting memories in a glass jar of several layers of coloured salt. This crystallizes special events and particular memories that each person has. The work on clay sculptures in subsequent sessions allowed for positive and future thinking: a life without special people but incorporating their memories and presence in other ways.

Although we were unable to meet with Peter's father, the family was able to talk about their activities with him, and involve him in their recovery progress. Peter especially was able to share with his father his memory box work, to include some of his dad's personal mementoes about his mother.

Outcomes

Meeting with the grandparents for one last session, we heard the good news that Peter was much more settled at home, and that they felt more confident in dealing with his aggressive outbursts as if he were any child and not one who had suffered such a tremendous loss. They better understood the way that young children do not always realize the permanence of someone dying, and how difficult they found it responding to Peter's constant questioning of 'When are they coming back?' The grandparents were able to reflect on their own processes, and their own struggles to come to terms with such tragic circumstances. The grandfather felt that he was able to acknowledge his need for further support, and we signposted him to bereavement agencies for ongoing individual work.

The SENCO and class teacher reported that Peter was happier in school, and they saw more glimpses of a very likeable little boy, who needed consistent and firm boundaries, similar to the other children in his class. His spitting had stopped and he was coming to school much calmer. Anger and aggressive outbursts were symptoms of Peter's anxieties, and as everyone around him became more confident and reassured that they were doing and saying the 'right' things, so Peter himself became less anxious.

The tangible outcomes had been met: the grandparents felt more able to understand and deal with Peter's tantrums and outbursts; both the school and family were encouraged to realize the different developmental aspects of grieving; and Peter felt held and supported by his family and school with appropriate strategies.

Both the school and Peter's family benefited from the support that we offered in understanding that children grieve 'in puddles', jumping in and out of sorrow and happiness, switching from one to the other alarmingly quickly. The confidence to experience fun and laugh again is a normal and expected 'stage', as well as the revisiting of the depth of sad emotions.

In this case the elephant in the room was not so much the parent missing from the therapy room as actually from the child's life itself. The fact remains, however, that, without access to the home and support for the grandparents in their grief, Peter would have been much more difficult to help.

Mutual benefits of joint working

In this particular history of joint working it may be said, therefore, that the inclusion of family therapy extended the practice of dramatherapy by setting it within a wider communication system. Whereas the stimulus and response was hitherto restricted to dramatherapist and child, it has now been broadened to involve the extra dynamics inherent in the family. Additionally, for the family therapist working alongside a dramatherapist, there has been an opportunity to see the family situation from the important perspective of the child. Just as dramatherapy needs family therapy to widen the picture and add the missing piece of the child's background, so family therapy benefits from a dramatherapist working with a child, in that the missing piece was previously that of the voice of the child. In the words of a family therapist, 'Family therapy needs dramatherapy because children find it difficult to say what they really feel in front of their parents.' Thus when a drama and family therapist visit a child and his family in the home, having previously worked separately with each, a scenario is set up whereby the child is empowered to speak and be heard: the child has the back-up of the dramatherapist who is already 'in the know'. Sometimes, if the session revolves around play, the whole process may remain within the land of metaphor, thus providing a sense of safety and containment for child and parent alike. Sometimes too, when metaphor through play is used, the sense of empowerment for the child is further enhanced in that they are already used to working in this way and are often then in the unusual position of being in control. This can also be a useful diagnostic tool, as explained in the section 'The power of playfulness' on p.144.

Examples of practical application

In order to give a fuller explanation of the joint working relationship of drama and family therapy, some general examples of its practical application will now be offered, before focusing on more specific accounts in the form of authentic case studies.

Although there may be other and possibly more effective examples of joint practice, it has been found that this particular working relationship functions best practically when the dramatherapist conducts a number of assessment sessions with the child while the family therapist meets with the family or primary carer. The drama and family therapists then come together to form one or more hypotheses of the situation and to reflect on a possible future intervention, either again separately or jointly.

For example, 'the child brings the family to therapy' is an often-used expression to denote the way a child is sometimes the barometer for their family. In other words, although it is the child who may be giving cause for concern by his behaviour, this is often his way of drawing attention to the fact that there is a cause for concern within the family. A case in point is the way a child may exhibit disturbing behaviour that has a direct correlation to the mental health issues of his primary carer. In other words, it is not the child who actually has the problem. This correlation is a difficult issue to unravel without the more diverse approach of a multi-agency team, and in particular the close relationship of a dramatherapist, who can work with the child, and the family therapist, who can work with the primary carer.

CASE STUDY: JANE – PROJECTION

Background

The request for involvement stated that Jane, aged ten, had a very negative view of herself, her school work, her life and her family, that made her very miserable. She was often quoted as saying that she didn't like to be positive about anything. Jane's class teacher found her to be fussy and distracting in class, often blaming others for any misdemeanours in which she was involved herself. Although bright and articulate, Jane seemed to have a 'negative confidence' that was puzzling for staff to respond to. She was described as sometimes having a sense of humour and ability to reflect on her feelings if she was in a good mood, but that didn't happen very often.

Jane lived at home with her mother and younger brother; their father had never lived with them, although he supported his children financially, and lived alone elsewhere in the country. Jane and her brother visited him, but they did not stay for any length of time, returning to the care of their mother earlier than expected. Mum did not contact the school very much, hardly attending any school events or parent evenings. Jane said very little about her home life, other than saying she was always in trouble at home.

The SENCO was concerned that Jane was not reaching her full potential academically and that her unhappiness was becoming a barrier to her learning. The tangible outcomes requested that Jane had access to some therapeutic support to enable her to have a more positive view of herself, to help her understand the areas of her life that caused her unhappiness, and to reduce the amount of time she spent distracting others in class.

Intervention

It was decided that, as family therapist, I would be the key worker to try to engage with Jane's family while my dramatherapist colleague gave Jane individual one-to-one support. Initially, it was difficult to contact Jane's mother and arrange a meeting time. However, a meeting was eventually organized, and it became apparent at that first session that Jane's mother Sue was very unwell and that she depended on Jane, as a girl, to care for her a lot of the time at home. Sue, after being somewhat reluctant to engage, began to talk about herself and her difficult relationship with Jane. A contract of work was agreed, and over several sessions Sue was able to describe how Jane was quite opinionated, unmotivated and unhappy, with no respect for her. Sue did not seem so negative when describing Jane's younger brother, and, although she found it very difficult to think of any positive words to describe Jane, she was able to express her dismay that Jane did not want to talk to her at all, and she was at a loss as to know what to do next.

Further sessions turned to understanding Sue herself. Her own early life had been harsh and bereft of warmth; she had spent some time in a children's home. Sue had been expected to care for her own mother, and as the eldest girl, it was her duty to do so. Sue had always found it hard to relate to others, and had what she described as an 'arm's length' relationship with the children's father, never living together. Sue seemed to have underlying issues with dependency, desperate for support but eliciting complex responses from others. Untangling some of her early experiences, Sue was able to come to some understanding and awareness of projecting onto Jane feelings of resentment and despair. She was then able to identify experiences of loss, a grieving for the loss of youth and adolescence.

Jane's work through dramatherapy was painstakingly slow. Although as a keen artist Jane was eager to engage in the sessions, initially she spent much time drawing fierce-looking animals and very little else. After some sessions of doing this, Jane began to talk through her drawings, but the emotions she expressed and the stories she told appeared to have little connection to reality.

The dramatherapist began to wonder where all this was coming from, since her understanding of Jane's home life and her relationship with her mother, although not good, did not seem to bear any relation to the violence and feelings of self-loathing which were coming out in the sessions. Why Jane felt this way was initially a mystery, and issues of child protection had to be eliminated before the possibility that the emotions were not Jane's but her mother's could be considered. We began working on the hypothesis that the child was dealing with feelings that were projected on to her by her mother.

In further joint sessions, both the dramatherapist and I were able to share some of the difficult emotions that had been voiced by Sue and Jane about each other, and to begin to support some changes in the way that they related. Sue was able to begin to praise Jane, and seek support for herself from other adults with similar ailments in a local support group. Having a focus and particular aim for each session meant that the small steps were achievable; for example, deciding that Jane could go out with a friend for a short period after school and negotiating between them for how long that would be.

Through creating small goals, changes were created in the way that Sue and Jane related that did not involve dependency issues. The work ended with a session that involved creative activities in which both Sue and Jane excelled and which they could share together, making small steps towards beginning to respect each other.

Outcomes

Jane had begun to have a different relationship with her mother that was more positive and somewhat happier. Jane did not distract others in class as much and her sense of humour was much more in evidence. Her teacher reported that Jane was engaging more with her learning, and that she was on task to reach her academic potential. However, Sue's complex needs were beyond the work of multi-agency support, and she was able to begin a contract of work with a counselling agency, something that she had been unable to even think about previously. Through counselling work, the underlying projection of attributing characteristics that she was unable to accept in herself would be dealt with in more depth.

The tangible outcomes were limited in being met, because Jane's home circumstances were still difficult and caregiving was still an ongoing issue. Jane certainly had a more positive view of herself that was being maintained by the supportive school staff. Learning mentor support was provided in school for Jane, to support ongoing self-confidence and self-esteem work. The exiting process with the school involved the suggestion that a further request for involvement could be made if necessary in the future.

Similarly, a child who is exhibiting incomprehensible and worrying behaviour following the loss of a member of the family may be supported to some extent by the dramatherapist working on bereavement issues. However, the picture will only be complete and the specific behaviour pattern addressed when, through the family therapist, it is learnt that this is exactly the way the child's father has behaved and that the issue here is not so much one of bereavement as of learnt behaviour. This was what happened in Michael's case: he took to hiding away under chairs in much the same way as his father refused, after the death of his brother, to go out of the house.

Sometimes, in addition to the psychodynamic work undertaken separately and jointly by drama and family therapists, it will become apparent that a more cognitive behavioural approach is also needed.

The use of behavioural charts, goal setting and contracts becomes much easier when lines of communication have been opened effectively with child and family alike.

CASE STUDY:
BEN – VOICES IN THE HEAD

Background

An eight-year-old child named Ben was referred to the multi-agency support team with concerns about his 'very strange' behaviour. Ben lived alone with his mum and had done since his father had left some years before. There had been a level of domestic violence that Ben had witnessed, but the details were hazy, since it was hard to pin down either Ben or his mum to facts. Mum was beginning to find Ben unmanageable in the home; they lived in a small flat on an inner city housing estate with their two dogs and a cat. The major concern, however, had come from school, where staff had reported Ben displaying some disturbing behaviour. According to the classroom assistant, Ben was often spiteful to other children and found it difficult to mix. The most worrying aspect, however, was that Ben frequently talked about strange things and had, on occasion, been violent towards his classmates, threatening to stab out their eyes or drill a hole in their brains with a pencil. When asked why, he just said that the voices in his head had told him to do this and showed little or no remorse, and seemed surprised that he had been asked, as if this sort of behaviour were normal. According to his teachers, there were also times when he appeared 'spaced out', and slightly vacant.

Ben was a bright boy, good at literacy and numeracy, and very good at comprehension and making up stories. This last appeared to be one of the problems, since Ben could never be trusted to tell the truth and was constantly inventing long, complicated tales about the reasons for his behaviour. One of these involved the 'wires in his brain' that made him do things.

Tangible outcomes requested that the threatening behaviour ceased, that Ben be able to mix better with his peers and that his mum be able to manage Ben better at home.

Intervention

The case was assigned to me as the dramatherapist on the team with a view to my working with Ben to discover the cause of these 'voices in the head'. A primary mental health worker had already made an assessment and, although she did not consider him to be of serious risk to himself or others, it was agreed that his behaviour was distressing enough for staff and peer group alike for him to be put on a waiting list for CAMHS. Meanwhile it was arranged that I would see Ben for dramatherapy sessions and my family therapist colleague would meet with his mum.

Ben presented as a very bright, talkative child, showing no fear of me or reluctance to engage. During the sessions it became apparent that there was much confusion for him around fact and fantasy. After a few weeks we divided the room into two and, on the red side, we played through the stories (mostly horror) that Ben told me he had seen on television. This was the fantasy or fibs side. I took care that Ben never strayed over to the other side of the room while playing through these themes. On the blue side we sat and mostly talked, taking it in turns, telling one thing which we *knew* to be true. This was the fact side. After a few sessions it became clear that, due to the domestic violence Ben had witnessed, there was overlapping subject matter between the two areas.

This was confirmed by my family therapy colleague who also discovered that Mum, because of her past experiences, kept the television on all night and that Ben copied her. At last there was a possible explanation for the 'wires in the brain' that made him do things.

Since this technique of separating fact from fantasy seemed to be working for Ben, it was referred on to the school, in particular Ben's teacher and classroom assistant, who, every time Ben started to tell them an impossible story, would reply with 'Is this from the red or the blue side?' Ben thought it all a huge joke, but gradually began to respond, and the violent threats and strange behaviour diminished.

In addition, my colleague had been supporting Mum in the home and gently building on her self-confidence. Mum had been the subject of an abusive relationship with Ben's father, and had had very little support at the time from her family. Through several sessions of one-to-one work, she was able to become aware of the courage and bravery that she had shown in starting a new life for herself and Ben. Using a solution-focused approach, Mum was able to understand that some of the aspects of her interactions with Ben were coming from a place of strength and that, at times, she coped very well. The therapeutic work encouraged her to do more of what she did well. For instance, both she and Ben shared a great sense of humour, and both were able to manage certain difficult interactions through making things seem funny.

Mum's confidence had been undermined by her previous relationship. She found it hard to be trusting and was initially suspicious of the support. She was quite chaotic in keeping appointments and maintaining house rules for Ben, but eventually, as her confidence grew, so Ben began to respond in a positive way. Another aspect of the intervention focused on how she coped with blips: that she wasn't 'going back to square one', and that her confidence wouldn't be destabilized.

Mum not only found it hard to understand the impact of what adult computer games and the constant playing of the television at night might have on Ben, but also to separate this from her own needs in the situation. However, since she wanted changes in the home environment and because of the improvement in Ben's behaviour at school, she was willing to make some changes herself.

Since there was some improvement in Ben's behaviour at school, we decided to focus on further therapeutic intervention in the home. My colleague and I met with Ben and his mum at home and were able to praise Ben for his improved behaviour at school in front of Mum. This began the session well, and Mum began to see Ben in a new light. Together we discussed the necessity for appropriate television and computer game usage, and Mum agreed to try to manage without her TV at night if Ben would do the same. We drew up a contract that both Mum and Ben signed, much to Ben's delight. Building on this new rapport between Ben and Mum, we then invited them to make some house rules. It was apparent that, as a growing boy, Ben was becoming bored and frustrated with his life in a small flat, so we suggested that, if Ben obeyed certain rules of Mum's, such as going to bed without a fuss and switching off the computer when asked, she would take him to the park every day after school. In addition we contacted the educational welfare officer on the team who was able to access some local clubs and societies, and Mum agreed, if Ben kept his part of the bargain, to take him. All this was put into writing on charts that adorned the walls of the flat.

Outcomes

The first tangible outcome had been met after a few weeks when Ben took to the 'fibs and facts' game and voluntarily began his own restorative process. More individual dramatherapy sessions were necessary for Ben to play through, process and appropriately allocate to fantasy or fact the violence he had witnessed. Ben was a typical example of a child whose cognitive abilities were not yet sufficiently developed for him to be able to adequately process abstract concepts. The violence he witnessed on screen was as real to him as the violence he had witnessed at home. All night long, through the television, images, sometimes disturbing, were speaking to his unconscious, and his unconscious processes were not becoming clarified, but mystified.

The second outcome needed a little more in the way of behavioural support since Ben had already earned himself a reputation of being 'strange' with his peers. The team's learning mentor was asked to work with Ben in a small group of his peers, and Ben's 'street cred' gradually improved as the group began to value his stories as creative and imaginative rather than strange.

The intervention put in at home met at first with intermittent success as both Mum and Ben found it difficult to keep to their contracts. Several home visits were necessary, but eventually, even though Ben continued to push boundaries, Mum was able to allow him more freedom in the way of attending clubs and time out on his skateboard, so that Ben's ever-exuberant energy had some other outlet.

With the tangible outcomes met, the team exited the case although aware that, due to the fragility of the home circumstances, a need for re-referral might arise at some date in the future. The referral to CAMHS was no longer deemed necessary. Although psychodynamic work had been needed to help Ben use the 'fibs and facts' technique to distinguish between fantasy and reality, the behavioural approach was necessary as a way of measuring and maintaining the progress made.

The power of playfulness

Although some therapists, for example Jim Wilson (2005) and Dan Hughes (2007, 2009), focus on play as a medium through which to facilitate the family's process, on the whole it may be safe to say that, up to now, play has been more the province of the dramatherapist rather than the family therapist. The coming together of a family and dramatherapist who involve their family in play therefore offers a unique and potentially powerful process. As previously mentioned, although the child may feel at home with this way of working, for the parents it may present a situation that they have not experienced, since they were children themselves. For an increasing number, brought up on computer games, it may even be a situation they have *never* experienced, which will, consequently, be viewed with extreme apprehension. Nevertheless, it is our experience that, with gentle encouragement, these parents can be persuaded to become involved in such activities as drawing or painting a rose garden or making a clay island with their offspring (Liebmann 1999). Here, the power lies in metaphor, which can be a useful diagnostic tool when one considers such questions as 'Who will you allow to visit your island?', 'Is there a wall around your garden?' and 'Does the plant you choose to be have thorns?'

CASE STUDY:
DYLAN – PAST SEXUAL ABUSE

Background

The request for involvement to the multi-agency support panel indicated that Dylan was a likeable seven-year-old boy, whose teacher noted that he seemed articulate, confident and clever, with a lovely smile and a great sense of humour. However, recently in school Dylan had shown signs of becoming very defiant, with a misplaced and inappropriate 'answer for everything' attitude. He was somewhat forgetful and disorganized, often mislaying books and school kit, but according to him it was never his fault, and he often gave quite complicated and evasive explanations for any misdeeds. The SENCO reported that Dylan was gaining a manipulative reputation in school, trying to change boundaries and verbally challenging staff. At times when he had become angry in class there did not seem to be a discernible pattern or explanation for his outbursts. Although Dylan enjoyed having lots of friends, he appeared to engage more productively with his schoolwork when working alone, and found group work difficult.

Dylan's mother Julie was a very young mum, separated from Dylan's father and with a new older partner, Jim, whose presence was very erratic in their lives. Dylan saw his father, Wayne, regularly at weekends, joining several other children in a busy chaotic household, very different to his somewhat solitary existence during the week at home with his mum. The split between Dylan's parents had not been amicable, and they differed in their views on how to parent him. Julie had come into school to request support because Dylan was not easy to manage at home and he was bedwetting nearly every night, although this did not seem to be the case when he was staying with his father.

The tangible outcomes requested that the parents work together to understand Dylan's needs, to gain a clearer understanding of the issues underlying the bedwetting, and support Dylan in changing his poor attitude towards his mother and other adults.

Intervention

The case was assigned to me as a family therapist on the team to be key worker, with a view to my working with Dylan's parents to understand and support their endeavours to parent him, and for my dramatherapist colleague to work initially on a one-to-one basis with Dylan to help unravel his difficulties and understand his underlying anxieties.

A meeting was arranged to meet with Julie and Wayne, but because of the tension between them this proved problematic, and it was agreed that contact with the parents would be on a separate basis, and consequently the central focus of the family therapy work would be with the residential parent Julie and her 'off–on' boyfriend Jim. An agreement was reached that Wayne would be kept informed of the general progress of the therapeutic work.

The contract of work of six weekly sessions with Julie was agreed and that the work would take place at home, where she lived with Dylan. The initial two sessions with Julie were tense, and as a therapist it was difficult to establish a therapeutic alliance and gain her trust. Julie experienced disapproval from Dylan's father of her parenting style, her choice of partner, and helping him with his schoolwork. Julie was unable to deal with her distress about what might have happened to Dylan in the past, as well as her own difficulties with past relationships. She seemed anxious about her relationship with Jim, and his elusiveness. An emotional connection and engagement with the therapeutic process was established with Julie by concentrating on the sense of purpose in achieving some small goals around house rules and boundaries at home that would help in understanding the underlying difficulties in Dylan's behaviour. After some success in this area, Julie felt more confident in her ability to manage Dylan's outbursts, giving him some limited choices in house rules whilst she kept 'overall command'. Their relationship improved, and Julie was able to begin to reveal more about her own personal difficulties.

During subsequent one-to-one sessions with Julie, through constructing a genogram and in life-line work, emotional and historical information was gained, and reflective work revealed past patterns and influences. Julie was able to understand her own abusive family history and the influence of drug abuse that was prevalent for some of her previous relationship partners, and including her present boyfriend, Jim. Through open and circular questioning, past conflicts and difficulties for Julie with various family members were brought to the sessions, so that she was able to understand how these events shaped her and her intimate interactions. Reframing and scaffolding techniques enabled Julie to understand how past problems had prevented her from becoming who she wanted to be, and helped her discover possible new outcomes. As Julie gained in confidence she was able to respond to future perspective questions, such as 'what if...?', and, subsequently, she revealed her fears about her present relationship.

The contract of work was extended, and other team members became involved, a police officer and family liaison officer, to help support an extraction from her situation, and her wish to end her relationship with Jim.

Alongside the work with Julie, Dylan was receiving one-to-one therapeutic support from my dramatherapist colleague. In the very first session Dylan identified with a baby tiger soft toy and played extensively with this and a bigger tiger toy. It became apparent that, for Dylan, there were many issues around boundaries, trust and feelings of safety. In accordance with her contract of confidentiality with Dylan, the dramatherapist relayed to me her concerns about his process, which I, in turn, was able to share with his mother. It was evident that for some reason Dylan was feeling unsafe, especially in the family home, and did not appear to be able to trust in his mother's ability to keep him safe.

Superficially there appeared to be an anomaly with the current situation in the home, since it was obvious that Dylan was Julie's overriding concern and he was never allowed out of her sight or alone with anyone else except his grandparents. In further discussion, however, it came to light that there had been an incident of sexual abuse for Dylan at a pre-verbal age by an ex-boyfriend of Julie's, and it was the dramatherapist's view that Julie's relationship with someone with whom Dylan did not feel entirely comfortable was triggering half-remembered emotions which he did not fully understand and was not able to put into words. These emotions were giving rise to unconscious anxiety, manifesting in the bedwetting and angry outbursts.

Understanding the possible reasons for Dylan's behaviour and knowing that he was being supported, Julie was able to cope in new ways with the adverse family reactions to the changes that she had made to her life.

With just Julie and Dylan living together, and with new insight and understanding about Dylan's difficulties, the therapeutic input became joint working with them both, meeting for a further four sessions with myself and the dramatherapist. The work centred on playfulness, encouraging Julie to be less anxious and meet her child on a level he could understand and enjoy. This included some board and card games that involved discussions about feelings, emotions and strengths, as well as the artistic creation of a rose garden and pirate island where such issues as safety and security could be explored in a 'fun' way through metaphor.

Outcomes

Dylan's bedwetting had stopped, the relationship between Julie and Dylan had improved, and their home life was more settled. Julie was able to assist in Dylan's recovery from past trauma by dealing with her own issues and becoming more robust herself.

Whilst Julie and Wayne had begun to present a more united front as parents, there was still a fundamental disagreement between them about how to deal with Dylan's disorganization and testing of boundaries. Both parents were able to agree that Dylan perhaps was seeking reassurance from them both, and they compromised, recognizing their differences but also recognizing that calm, clear and consistent boundaries that worked in school could be utilized at home. Both parents agreed to give Dylan more respect and responsibility for his own behaviour when staying at each of their homes, with the different styles. As they changed, so did Dylan. The tangible outcomes had been met, and while Dylan still reacted to high stress levels and tension in family and school life with challenging responses, these were managed in a way that met Dylan's needs.

In this way the relationship between a parent (or carer) and child can be explored in an entirely non-threatening way with some occasionally surprising results. For example, Hannah, a young girl who had presented as being neglected and possibly emotionally abused by her mother, was seen in a joint session to be very much the one in control. The 'victim' role, which was one her mother often played outside the family, was echoed by the child in interactions with her teachers and peers. Both mother and child had found this dysfunctional role served a purpose, and a complicated enmeshment situation had developed. Further work involved making puppets to decide who was pulling whose strings and why.

The effectiveness of involving parent (or, if possible, parents) and child in playful activities is paramount when considering issues of attachment. The vital components which make up healthy early attachment such as a mother mirroring the smile, first words and gestures of her baby can be revisited through the therapist acting as role model for the parent during the sessions. As suggested in the section 'How does it work in education?' on p.44, if this important early stage of development is somehow missed, then it will need to be revisited and reworked (or replayed), not only for the child but also for the parent, until the bonds of trust are in place.

CASE STUDY:
ALICE – ATTACHMENT

Background

Alice, nearly nine years old, seemed to have a catalogue of problems when she was referred to the multi-agency support team, and an array of support had already been implemented for her. The request for involvement described her as aggressive, both physically and verbally, towards her peers, often displaying defiant and disruptive behaviour in class. Although craving adult attention, she did not always understand social cues and the feelings of others, seeming very demanding at all times. Her class teacher thought that Alice's moods were very unpredictable, and said that, although she could be considerate to others, at other times she seemed very contrary and unhappy.

The main concern was that Alice was not reaching her learning potential. It was, as her teacher reported, 'all very puzzling' and difficult to understand exactly what the triggers were for her oppositional behaviour. In addition, her teacher described Alice as taking up a lot of her time and guidance in class, to the detriment of other children. Although Alice seemed to find girls easier to get on with than boys, she often played on the periphery of school break-time games and did not seem to have any close friends.

Alice was an only child and lived with her single-parent mother; her father had disappeared soon after Alice was born and no one knew his whereabouts. Mum (Kerry) and Alice lived close to the maternal grandparents, who were becoming increasingly dependent on their daughter. Kerry had asked for help because she was finding it difficult to get Alice into school on time some days, and she was at a loss to deal with Alice's point-blank refusal to comply with getting ready in the mornings.

The inclusion office reported that previous assessment of Alice by CAMHS had revealed emotional delay, but was not aware of the nature of the support offered at the time. Alice had previously been assessed by the Communication Interaction Team (CIT), who did not find any problems and reported that her levels of communication reached the required developmental criteria. Although judged to be lacking in empathy, she was not considered to require a Statementing process by the school educational psychologist. She did, however, have an Individual Educational Plan (IEP) to support her learning and behaviour.

The tangible outcomes for the request for involvement to the multi-agency support team were for Alice to be able to achieve her potential, to manage her feelings better, and for her to fit in better with her class cohorts.

Intervention

The case was assigned to me as the family therapist to be key worker, primarily to work with Kerry at home to understand more about her desire for support. My dramatherapist colleague would work with Alice to discover her needs and help unlock the 'puzzle'.

Over a period of six sessions I met with Kerry and discovered that, although she was talkative, she was very flat and unemotional in her responses. Kerry indicated that she was not taking any medication, but had been to her GP because she felt low, although she said he had not been particularly helpful. In the first session, she described how being a parent was very scary, and that she had received little support from anyone during Alice's early years. Her own mother had become infirm when she was young, and her father, Alice's grandfather, had been suffering from ill health for many years, becoming increasingly dependent. Alice had been a 'good baby', but Kerry seemed somewhat detached and distant when outlining her story. The few times that Kerry showed some depth of emotion was in her depiction of Alice's father, who she denoted as jealous of Alice, and as having vanished as soon as he could.

Through narrative therapy during subsequent sessions, Kerry was able to recognize and externalize her anger. She expressed surprise at how well she had survived on her own with so little support. Describing her own life story, Kerry revealed that family communication and interactions had been very limited, and attachments to others were not encouraged. As the youngest of several siblings she was expected to get on with things, particularly when her mother became unwell when she, Kerry, was ten years old. Through encouragement and tentative examples, Kerry was able to tell her life story as being one of seriousness, without much joy, with the subtext that it was not a good idea to be too close to anyone.

Kerry had found it hard to bond emotionally with Alice, other than on what appeared to be a surface level, and was at a loss to know what triggered her 'moods'. They both, however, had a physical dependency on each other, since Alice was still sleeping in Kerry's bed. Additionally, Kerry was very protective of Alice, in that she blamed the school for not understanding her better.

Through providing a secure base for the therapeutic alliance, we were able to explore and understand some of Kerry's own early formative bonds, the nature of which had influenced her further relationships. Kerry was able to reflect that her unemotional presentation was difficult for Alice to understand, and that perhaps Alice was anxious about leaving her mother at home looking after the grandparents.

Meanwhile Alice was meeting with the dramatherapist on a weekly basis with a view to using drama and story work (which Alice loved) as a medium through which her already-diagnosed emotional delay could be explored. During these sessions it became apparent that there was a mismatch between the level of Alice's cognitive and emotional development. An emotional 'neediness' seemed to underpin most of her work, as was graphically displayed in her story of the little tiger, whose mummy was prevented from finding and helping him by a big, big dragon.

After the individual sessions were complete, the work became a joint venture, and my dramatherapist colleague and I met with both Kerry and Alice at school after lessons had ended for the day. We played board games that encouraged emotional expression and took part in role plays, dressing up in many different materials so that bonding between Mum and child was gained through fun. Through these joint interventions, new narratives and storytelling could be explored, providing fertile ground for different ways of communicating feelings.

Outcomes

We kept in close contact with the class teacher throughout, who reported that Alice was generally accessing her learning in more productive ways. The IEP was adapted to include some of the new understanding around Alice's difficulties. Alice found boys noisy, school assembly unbearable, and playtimes tricky, and the class teacher was able to re-evaluate Alice's behaviour during those times and be more accommodating, rather than seeing Alice as naughty. Kerry had become more self-aware and was able to value herself more, insisting that one of her siblings take a more active part in caring for their parents. She was consequently able to manage morning routines better, and Alice arrived at school more settled and less anxious. Her aggressive outbursts were not so frequent, although her emotional development is an ongoing process. As the bond between mother and child improved, both became less anxious about each other, and Alice was able to take more independent steps, for example sleeping in her own bed, with the result that they were able to share the shopping and the decorating of Alice's 'new' bedroom.

Through utilizing different strategies in class, Alice's teacher was able to encourage her to be more relaxed and, because her outbursts lessened, her cohorts were less wary and included Alice more in their games. However, friendships were still a problem, and learning mentor group work support around social stories was initiated by the school inclusion officer. Nevertheless, the rest of the class were more able to focus on their learning, and experienced less disruption from Alice as she became 'more like one of the others'.

Since the tangible outcomes had been met, the team exited the case, although Alice was still not a 'perfect' child at home or at school. Both mother and child had come a long way in their understanding of each other and of their place in the outside world, and even though it was agreed that further intervention might be necessary at a later date, it was felt everyone had a better grasp of Alice and her emotional needs.

Issues to consider

Although, as we have seen, joint working has many benefits for therapists and clients alike, one potential hazard to be aware of is the danger of polarization. Obviously, if a dramatherapist has been working with a child, allowing him to tell his story at his own pace, and gently entering his world, then she may struggle at some point to remain completely objective. The same may also be true for the family therapist, especially if she is working with a lone parent. The need for supervision from a third party then becomes imperative in order to sort out the possible transference and countertransference issues. As Sue Jennings explains, 'Transference is the human propensity to transfer feelings that belong to people in our past experience to people we encounter in the present' (Jennings 1990, p.11). For example, as in Hannah's case, it was necessary for our supervisor to point out to Penny that her 'damaged' child was speaking to the rescuer in her in much the same way the mother was to her family therapist colleague.

In conclusion, the joint working of drama and family therapy may be seen as valuable support for children and their families. In this particular multi-agency set-up, an ideal scenario might be, for example, for the therapists to be working with the child and family while an educational psychologist looks at classroom behaviour, an educational welfare officer gives help in getting the child to school on time and a police liaison officer offers crucial background information if necessary, and support for older – potentially youth offending – siblings. In this scenario, the therapy team have the unique opportunity of being able to use various techniques to understand their clients 'from the inside out'. This, together with the interventions mentioned above, which, on the whole, address the needs 'from the outside in', forms an integrated and holistic picture of the whole issue from assessment through to intervention.

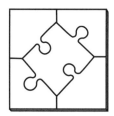

CONCLUSION

A whole is that which has a beginning, middle and end.
[Aristotle]

WHY THERAPY WITHIN THE MULTI-AGENCY APPROACH WORKS

Usefulness to the child

In the desire to address the needs of the child from every single angle available within a multi-agency context, there can be a tendency to evaluate those needs, not from the child's perspective, but from the adult's. Liaising with different disciplines and agencies is adult work, and while it is very necessary, the ensuing network of communications can become a complexity in which the child's voice is lost.

Allowing the child a voice is the job of the dramatherapist, who has the luxury of being able to meet with that child without any of the preconceptions attributed to him by virtue of his environment, parental upbringing, academic or emotional development, and so on. As we have seen, she can start from where he is and allow him to tell her, either in a conversation built on trust or through the metaphor of his play, his version of events: his take on why he may be behaving in such a way.

A drama (or other creative arts) therapist has the unique opportunity of setting the stage for the child and allowing him the time and the space to find out for himself how he feels about his problems. This is a very different approach to a more behaviourally oriented one in which the reasons for the behaviour are generally pre-diagnosed and strategies of intervention already laid out. This sort of approach addresses the cognitive, reasoning faculties of the child's mind and is a very useful tool in implementing and maintaining, among other aspects, models of good behaviour for a child.

So, too, is the increasingly popular technique of cognitive behavioural therapy, with its emphasis on forming positive neural pathways in the brain. It is our opinion that there is a place for all approaches in supporting a child with emotional and behavioural difficulties, and that an ideal situation would perhaps be one where there could be a marrying of the varying disciplines in the effort to bring about the best possible assessment of, and intervention for, the troubled child.

Having said this, it also remains our opinion that the presence of a creative arts therapist on a multi-agency team is a unique and essential opportunity for that team to gain access to the unblemished mind of the child. Acting alone, the dramatherapist has only limited powers to achieve a sustainable difference for the child, which is why recourse to and liaison with a family therapist can potentially bring about the desired results in terms of long-lasting improvements to the life of the child and the family as a whole.

In conclusion, therefore, the usefulness of therapy in a multi-agency team lies in the fact that, having met the child on his own terms and allowed him centre stage to play out his issues, the dramatherapist can then, with the child's permission, bring his perspective back to the team and her fellow family therapists. This then becomes an important piece of the jigsaw which throws light on the picture as a whole, from which a way ahead more appropriate to the child's needs may be planned.

Usefulness to the family

Bringing about long-lasting changes for the family as a whole requires meeting and understanding them and their needs within a therapeutic alliance. Allowing the family that space and working with interactions and relationships allows for the attention to focus on family-based issues. Evidence-based research and evaluation has recognized that working at a therapeutic level with the family offers the best way to provide the opportunity for sustained change. Different therapies offer support for the family to understand their level of need and to effect change, and systemic family therapy enables those changes to be maintained and built on. Increased understanding between family members, and between family and school, enables different ways of communicating, thinking and feeling. Working in depth and collaboratively with families, family therapists are able to hold the uniqueness of each individual person within the family, the complexity of the family unit, and the impact of cultural and social influences on the child and family.

The usefulness to the family is having someone 'on their side'; the therapist can more fully understand their perspective by meeting them on their terms, listening to their unique family stories, and understanding their point of view. Sometimes families, when immersed in a problem-saturated place, cannot see 'the wood for the trees'; they become stuck and feel blamed. Some families feel stigmatized and misunderstood; therapy offers the family an opportunity to reveal a different picture of itself, to have the concerns of the family members understood, and to give the family a voice.

The degree of trust that is an essential part of the relationship between the therapist and the family makes it more likely that a family will be able to share their worries about their child, and even give a voice to the strengths that exist, often buried under a culture of culpability.

The non-expert stance of a therapeutic input is a refreshing aspect within perceived 'expert' members of the team. Therapy offers a chance to think about the context of family life and the patterns and cycles of communication that play out in the everyday situations at home to understand the deeper meaning of things. Children often feel supported when their parents are helped to address their own issues, enabling family life to become more relaxed and not so hostile. The interpersonal level of therapy is particularly effective for the family, using as it does the focus of interpersonal techniques to address emotional and behavioural problems.

The therapeutic stance is useful for the family in terms of the 'not knowing' that allows the family to explain their own sense of what it is to 'know' them and their present difficulties. How they find themselves in their predicament and how they see things are an important aspect in the search for solutions and alternative ways of managing concerns and difficulties. Therapy for families, using their language to understand their complexities, is a support that is less intrusive than other interventions that they might have experienced. As with children, families need acknowledgement of how they sometimes cope with immense difficulties; therapy is therefore key in ensuring the family members are heard. The family perspective is an important part of the jigsaw and to the work of the team.

Usefulness to the team

Perhaps the most important aspect of therapeutic input to a multi-agency team is that it looks to answer the questions 'how?' and 'why?' rather than 'what?'. That is, obviously, not to say that other disciplines are not concerned with the reasons for the child's behaviour, but rather that the therapy team is primarily focused upon uncovering the issues that lead to the presenting problems.

This, in turn, is not to present an image of the therapists in question as a kind of amateur detective team. On the contrary, most therapists would be appalled at such a notion! Rather, it is, as has been said, the therapists' aim to set the stage in such a way that the child or the family discovers the reasons for, and causes of, their difficulties *themselves*. It is the nature of the work that both family and dramatherapists facilitate rather than direct the proceedings.

This, then, is different to the approach of other disciplines on the team where the skills and experience of the professionals concerned is brought to bear in considering how to solve the problem of the behaviour. For example, among other issues, the educational psychologist will look at how to help the child behave better in class or the school to manage him more effectively; the police liaison officer will look at strategies to prevent the child from offending in the wider community; and the learning mentor will aim to provide the support that child needs to raise his level of academic ability. It remains the province of the therapeutic team to address the emotional needs of the child and family from their perspective alone.

Bringing the therapy perspective to team discussions and deliberations about referrals or request for involvement is an important aspect for any decision making that the team decides upon. Different professionals talk about the same problem in different ways and often use 'a different language'. A therapeutic stance brings an enhancement to any team talks about children and their families, and a systemic view develops the holistic awareness in discerning ways forward. Every multi-agency team has its own identity and is made up of differing professional remits and skills. The usefulness of therapy is bringing a creative and reflective thread to the context of the team makeup and the rich mix of debates and ensuing work carried out with children, families and schools.

Usefulness to the school and wider community

In considering this particular aspect it might be helpful to look at drama and family therapy first as separate interventions before evaluating their joint impact on the above organizations. Historically, in our experience, schools have valued the presence of an arts therapist in their midst, since the support has been in the nature of a 'take out' rather than an 'add on'. By that we mean that the school refers the child, the therapist takes the child out of the classroom over a number of weeks, aims to 'sort him out', and then returns him to the class where he settles back in without further ado. This is obviously putting it in extremely crass terms, but is nevertheless the truth.

The school does not have to look at providing their own resources in the way of staffing to receive this support, and the child is not disrupting the class during the period of his therapy.

Having said this, most schools do not simply regard the therapeutic support as an easy way of getting rid of 'little Johnny' for an hour, but become involved out of interest and care for the child's well-being. Some schools even go so far as to encourage their staff to advance their knowledge of this particular intervention by arranging training sessions.

Having a drama or other creative arts therapist in school on a weekly basis also enables the school to view the child in an entirely different light. With the current pressure on schools to reach certain academic standards, it is difficult for them to contemplate the child's progress as other than how it is reflected in his schoolwork. Having an outside agency that considers the child from every angle *other* than his schoolwork offers the school a more holistic and valuable picture of that child.

Family therapy adds a further dimension to the view of the child held by the school, another angle when reflecting on barriers to learning. Each child and their family are unique, and understanding the challenges they face helps the school in dealing with any school-based problem. Families face pressures too in managing everyday life, and the child is influenced by these, as well as the pressures of school expectations. Family therapy supports the family unit in making changes, and is useful in helping the school have a greater understanding of the complexities of a particular family context.

Family therapists are able to bring the systemic understanding of both the family system and the school system, helping link the two in ways of supporting each other for the benefit of the child.

Schools benefit from creative and systemic therapy input in staff training and development for school professionals about the emotional and mental health issues of children. This helps promote a way of helping the early identification of those children most at risk of developing emotional difficulties, as well as supporting staff dealing with children with 'behaviour' issues. Often school-based interventions that have focused on children's behaviour have been based on reactive measures. Systemic thinking plays a part in supporting school professionals to work in more preventative and proactive ways, helping them think of alternative ways of dealing with any problems. A therapeutic dimension is a useful aspect on many different levels to schools and families, particularly in any meetings that take place between them.

As has been pointed out to us by schools on a number of occasions, one of the advantages of having the therapeutic team on board has been that there are very few agencies who either have statutory rights, or (as in this case) who are welcomed, to enter family homes. Parents asked to attend a meeting at school about their child's behaviour are often immediately on the defensive. Sometimes just having to come on to the school premises and meet with a teacher or headteacher is a huge ordeal in itself, and may bring back unwanted memories of their own childhood experiences. Under these circumstances schools often find parents less than co-operative. To meet with parents in their own homes and on their own terms can be much less intimidating (sometimes for all concerned!) and hence productive.

The school system is intimidating in many ways, and school life can be difficult for the family to understand. The complexities of a school day are just as distinct to a particular school as the day-to-day interactions of each unique family. In the same way, each community has a local identity, with a culture and ethnicity that in some ways might be intimidating to 'outsiders' or people from other parts of a town or city. A holistic approach helps the family and the school understand each other, and the fact that each has a 'life of their own' within the local community context. Therapeutic input and systemic views bring a multi-contextual aspect to the joint working of work in schools.

The joint intervention offered by a drama and family therapist may be said, therefore, to be of immense value to the school and the wider community, in that it places the child within the context of his environment and endeavours to provide an assessment of, and support for, his problems, which, more often than not, stem from that environment rather than the school itself.

Usefulness in a multi-cultural society

We have already discussed the fact that both dramatherapy and family therapy come from a stance that might be called 'non-expert'. Therefore, by allowing the child or family to be the experts with regards to their own healing and to express their own opinions, the therapists are adopting a non-prejudiced and non-judgemental attitude, which permits the freedom of expression and ideas so necessary when working in a multi-cultural setting.

Moreover, by focusing on relationships, the stories and narratives told and heard, and the metaphorical use of language, this kind of therapeutic intervention strikes at the heart of many difficulties experienced by those no longer living in their native country. Through using metaphor, which transcends the prescriptive parameters of language, and by working with archetypal themes, as relevant in Asia as in Europe, this sort of therapeutic work can be applicable the world over. As Strevitt Smith says of her work as part of a multi-disciplinary team in a multi-cultural setting, the same set of small-world objects can represent one thing to a family from Jamaica and something entirely different to a homesick girl and her aunty from Ghana (Strevitt Smith 2010). The objects themselves may be meaningless; their value lies in the extent to which, as objects of projection, they may become meaningful in entirely different ways to entirely different people.

It is not only through the therapeutic technique of projection that families from other countries are able to explore their feelings of displacement. Rehearsing social situations and finding more functional roles can be hugely helpful to families who find themselves in circumstances foreign to them. Humour, playfulness and creativity, intrinsic to the process of drama and family therapy, are very useful here in breaking down barriers and crossing cultural divides. Very often the therapy team can learn much from the family members as they explore how to remember and validate their own customs while finding out how to assimilate those of their new country.

In essence it is, as we have said, that belief in the innate capability of both child and family member to find within themselves, whatever that self is and to whatever society it belongs, the potential necessary for healing that makes drama and family therapy so effective in a multi-cultural society.

HOW THE PIECES INTERLOCK

The pieces of the jigsaw interlock through the multi-agency team format. Teams that have the courage to work across boundaries of skills while maintaining professionalism achieve greater multi-agency effectiveness. A team culture that celebrates creativity helps the pieces of a jigsaw come together, to enable the child, the family and the school to achieve sustainable and useful change. As this book illustrates, therapeutic principles help support the team players to interconnect to provide a cohesive package of support. Therapeutic interventions within the multi-agency approach support families in finding new ways to relate and 'stick' together, and therapy helps alleviate the suffering and anxieties that some children experience. Educationalists also appreciate the systemic approach of thinking about all the aspects of a child's life: in school, at home and in the community; in other words, the contextual elements of any circumstance or situation that make up the interlocking pieces.

Describing the pieces of the jigsaw in this book illustrates the flexibility, fluidity and versatility, as well as the professional commitment, that are the necessary core values and the 'glue' that connects all the parts together. Within a systemic ethos, as therapists we have not only been able to work jointly but also with other members of our team, providing a valuable service that has been useful to children, families, schools and the community.

MORE THAN THE SUM...

'The whole is more than the sum of its parts' is a misquoted saying attributed to Aristotle. Perhaps it is more appropriate to state that the whole is greater than the pieces, and each piece is necessary to make up the whole. Without the team we would not be able to meet with the child, family and school, and without those people we would not be able to practise in the way that we have demonstrated which is so incredibly useful and enjoyable.

In conclusion, it is our hope that we have succeeded in conveying through this book, not only the way that dramatherapy and family therapy work as separate disciplines, but also how they are able to work well together as well as within a multi-agency context. It is through the synergy of all the pieces that the jigsaw is completed and we are able to see the whole picture for what it really is. In this way, by taking what works best from our individual practices, we, as professionals, are able to join together to work for the best in providing an emotionally stable future for our children and our children's children.

REFERENCES

Anderson, T. (ed.) (1990) *The Reflecting Team*. New York: W.W. Norton.

Association for Family Therapy (AFT) (2011) *Code of Ethics and Practice: Ethics*. Available at www.aft.org.uk, accessed on 8 October 2011.

Baron-Cohen, S. (1995) *Mind Blindness: An Essay on Autism and Theory of Mind*. Cambridge, MA: MIT.

Bateson, G. (1972) *Steps to an Ecology of Mind: Mind and Nature*. New York: Ballantine Books.

Bowlby, J. (1988) *A Secure Base*. New York: Basic Books.

Boxall, M. (2002) *Nurture Groups in Schools: Principles and Practice*. London: Sage Publications.

British Association of Dramatherapists (2005) *Code of Practice: Boundaries*. Available at www.badth.org.uk/code, accessed on 20 February 2011.

British Association of Dramatherapists (undated) *Dramatherapy Page*. Available at www.badth.org.uk/dtherapy, accessed on 26 September 2011.

Brun, B. (1993) 'Symbols of the Soul: Fairy Tales.' In B. Brun, E.W. Pedersen and M. Runberg (eds) *Symbols of the Soul: Therapy and Guidance through Fairy Tales*. London: Jessica Kingsley Publishers.

Byng-Hall, J. (1995) *Re-Writing Family Scripts: Improvisation and Systems Change*. London: Guilford Press.

Byng-Hall, J. (2008) 'Crucial roles of attachment in family therapy.' *Journal of Family Therapy 30*, 129–146.

Caldwell Cook, H. (1917) *The Play Way: An Essay in Educational Method*. New York: F.A. Stokes Company.

Campbell, J. (2008) *The Hero with a Thousand Faces*. Novato, CA: New World Library.

Carr, A. (2000) 'Evidence-based practice in family therapy and systemic consultation.' *Journal of Family Therapy 22*, 273–295.

Carroll, L. (1993) *Alice in Wonderland*. Ware: Wordsworth Classics: Wordsworth Editions Ltd. (Original work published 1865.)

Carter, E. and McGoldrick, M. (1980) *The Family Life Cycle: A Framework for Family Therapy*. New York: Gardner Press.

Chazan, S. (2002) *Profiles of Play*. London: Jessica Kingsley Publishers.

Courtney, R. (1987) 'Dramatherapy and the Teacher.' In S. Jennings (ed.) *Dramatherapy: Theory and Practice 1*. London: Routledge.

Dallos, R. and Draper, R. (2000) *An Introduction to Family Therapy: Systemic Theory and Practice*. Maidenhead: Open University Press.

Department for Education and Skills (DfES) (2001) *Promoting Children's Mental Health within Early Years and School Settings*. London: DfES.

Department for Education and Skills (DfES) (2004) *Every Child Matters: Change for Children*. London: DfES.

Department for Education and Skills (DfES) (2006) *Permanent and Fixed Period Exclusions from Schools and Exclusion Appeals in England 2004/2005*. London: DfES.

Department of Health (DoH) (2005) *National Service Framework for Children and Young People: Executive Summary*. London: DoH.

De Shazer, S. (1982) *Patterns of Brief Therapy: An Ecosystemic Approach*. New York: Guilford Press.

Dowling, E. (1994) 'Taking the Clinic to the School: A Consultative Service for Parents, Children and Teachers.' In E. Dowling and E. Osborne (eds) *The Family and the School: A Joint Systems Approach to Problems with Children*. London: Karnac.

Dowling, E. and Osborne, E. (eds) (1994) *The Family and the School: A Joint Systems Approach to Problems with Children*. London: Routledge.

Dowling, E. and Osborne, E. (eds) (2003) *The Family and School: A Joint Systems Approach to Problems with Children*. London: Karnac.

Erikson, E.H. (1968) *Identity: Youth and Crisis*. New York: Norton.

Frith, U. (1989) *Autism: Explaining the Enigma*. Oxford: Basil Blackwell.

Gersie, A. and King, N. (1990) *Storymaking in Education and Therapy*. London: Jessica Kingsley Publishers.

Haley, J. (1976) *Problem Solving Therapy*. San Francisco, CA: Jossey Bass.

Hallam, S. (2007) 'Evaluation of behavioural management in schools: a review of the Behaviour Improvement Programme and the role of Behaviour and Education Support Teams.' *Association for Child and Adolescent Mental Health 12*, 3, 106–112.

Harvey, J. (2006) *What is a Child's Understanding of Family Therapy?* Master's thesis in Systemic Practice with Families and Couples, School of Psychology, University of Exeter.

Hoffman, L. (1988) *Foundations of Family Therapy*. New York: Basic Books.

Hughes, D. (2007) *Attachment-Focused Family Therapy*. New York: Norton Professional Books.

Hughes, D. (2009) *Principles of Attachment-Focused Parenting: Effective Strategies to Care for Children*. New York: Norton Professional Books.

Jennings, S. (1984) *Remedial Drama*. London: A&C Black.

Jennings, S. (1990) *Dramatherapy with Families, Groups and Individuals: Waiting in the Wings*. London: Jessica Kingsley Publishers.

Jennings, S. (1995) *Theatre, Ritual and Transformation: The Senoi Temiars*. London: Routledge.

Jennings, S., Cattanoch, A., Mitchell, S. and Meldrum, B. (1994) *The Handbook of Dramatherapy*. London: Routledge.

Johnson, D.W. and Johnson, F.P. (1997) *Joining Together: Group Theory and Group Skills*. London: Allyn and Bacon Publishers.

Jones, E. (2000) *Family Systems Therapy: Developments in the Milan-Systemic Therapies*. Chichester: Wiley.

Jung, C. (1978) *Man and his Symbols*. London: Picador. (Original work published 1964.)

Karkou, V. (2010) *Arts Therapies in Schools: Research and Practice*. London: Jessica Kingsley Publishers.

Kellermann, P.F. (2000) 'The Therapeutic Aspects of Psychodrama with Traumatized People.' In P.F. Kellermann and M.K. Hudgins (eds) *Psychodrama with Trauma Survivors*. London: Jessica Kingsley Publishers.

Lahad, M. (1992) 'Story-Making in Assessment Method for Coping with Stress: Six-Piece Story Making and BASICPh.' In S. Jennings (ed.) *Dramatherapy: Theory and Practice 2*. London: Routledge.

Lahad, M. (2000) *Creative Supervision*. London: Jessica Kingsley Publishers.

Landy, R. (1991) 'The dramatherapy role method.' *Journal of Dramatherapy 14*, 2, 7–15.

Landy, R. (1993) *Persona and Performance: The Meaning of Role in Dramatherapy and Everyday Life*. New York: Guilford Press.

Leigh, L., Dix, A., Gersch, I. and Haythorne, D. (2012) *Dramatherapy with Children, Young People and Schools: Enabling Creativity, Sociability, Communication and Learning*. London: Routledge.

Liebmann, M. (1999) *Art Therapy for Groups: A Handbook of Themes, Games and Exercises*. London: Routledge.

Lindsey, C. (2003) 'Some Aspects of Consultation to Primary Schools.' In E. Dowling and E. Osborne (eds) *The Family and the School: A Joint Systems Approach to Problems with Children*. London: Karnac.

Lippel, S. (2006) *Identity, Values and Power: An Investigation into Multi-Professional Team Working*. Doctorate thesis in Educational Psychology, University of Bristol.

McFarlane, P. (2005) *Dramatherapy: Developing Emotional Stability*. London: David Fulton Publishers.

Miller, P. (1983) *Theories of Developmental Psychology*. New York: W.H. Freeman Publishers.

Minuchin, S. (1974) *Families and Family Therapy*. Cambridge, MA: Harvard University Press.

Nichols, M.P. and Schwartz, R.C. (eds) (1998) *Family Therapy: Concepts and Methods* (4th edition). Needham Heights, MA: Allyn & Bacon.

Osborne, E. (2003) 'An Educational Psychologist's Perspective.' In E. Dowling and E. Osborne (eds) *The Family and the School: A Joint Systems Approach to Problems with Children*. London: Karnac.

Palazolli, M.S., Boscolo, L., Cecchin, G. and Prata, G. (1980) 'Hypothesizing–circularity–neutrality: three guidelines for the conductor of the session.' *Family Process 19*, 1, 3–12.

Piaget, J. (1970) 'Piaget's Theory.' In P.H. Mussen (ed.) *Carmichael's Manual of Child Psychology, Volume 1*. New York: John Wiley Publishers.

Reimers, S. and Treacher, A. (1995) *Introducing a User-Friendly Family Therapy*. London: Routledge.

Rivett, M. and Street, E. (2003) *Family Therapy in Focus*. London: Sage.

Rivett, M. and Street, E. (2009) *Family Therapy: 100 Key Points and Techniques*. London and New York: Routledge.

Safeguarding Children (2005) *Safeguarding Children: The Second Joint Chief Inspectors' Report on Arrangements to Safeguard Children*. Available at www.safeguardingchildren. org.uk/Safeguarding-Children/2005-report, accessed on 26 September 2011.

Slade, P. (1955) *Child Drama*. London: University of London Press.

Strevitt Smith, A. (2010) 'Dramatherapy in the context of systemic family therapy: Towards systmeic dramatherapy.' *Journal of the British Association of Dramatherapists 32*, 1, 8.

Tomm, M.D. (1988) 'Interventive interviewing: Part III. Intending to ask lineal, circular, strategic, or reflexive questions?' *Family Process 27*, 1, 1–15.

UK Council for Psychotherapy (UKCP) (2011) *Standards, Guidance and Policy Statements: Ethics*. Available at www.psychotherapy.org.uk/ukcp_standards_and_policy_statements.html, accessed on 9 October 2011.

Vetere, A. and Dowling, E. (eds) (2005) *Narrative Therapies with Children and Their Families*. Hove: Routledge.

Wagner, B.J. (1990) *Dorothy Heathcote: Drama as a Learning Medium*. Cheltenham: Stanley Thornes Publishers.

White, M. and Epston, D. (1990) *Narrative Means to Therapeutic Ends*. New York: W.W. Norton.

Wilson, J. (2005) 'Engaging Children and Young People: A Theatre of Possibilities.' In A. Vetere and E. Dowling (eds) *Narrative Therapies with Children and Their Families*. Hove: Routledge.

Winnicott, D.W. (1965) *The Maturational Process and the Facilitating Environment*. London: Hogarth Press.

SUBJECT INDEX

AUTHOR INDEX